Grammar I: Nouns, articles, and pronouns

Masculine and feminine nouns

- For nouns ending in **-o**, change the ending to **-a**:
  - Vecino → Vecina (neighbour)
  - Amigo → amiga (friend)
  - Maestro → Maestra (master)
- For nouns that end in **-or**, add **-a** to the ending:
  - Profesor → Profesora (teacher)
- For nouns that end in **-ente**, **-ante**, **-ista**, make no changes:
  - Estudiante (student)
  - Artista (artist)
  - Mente (mind)
- There is a general tolerance of the feminine version of professional titles. For example 'El jefe' has traditionally referred to both a male and female boss, but 'La jefa' with the **-a** ending is a more recent addition in the language. Other examples may include:
  - El doctor / La doctora (doctor)
  - El abogado / La abogada (lawyer)
  - El ingeniero / La ingeniera (engineer)
- There are certain nouns where the male and female versions do not translate equally, unlike the ones mentioned above, for example:
  - Hijo / Hija (son / daughter)
  - Hermano / Hermana (brother / sister)
  - Señor / Señora (Mister / Mrs.)

Plural nouns

- For nouns ending in a **vowel** (a, e, i, o, u), add **-s**.
- For nouns ending in a **consonant**, add **-es**.
- For nouns ending in **-z**, change to **-c**, and then add **-es**.
- For nouns ending in **-(i)ón**, add **-es** and drop the accent.

	Examples	
	Singular	Plural
Nouns ending in vowels	la casa (house)	las casas (houses)
	el amigo (friend)	los amigos (friends)
	la mano (hand)	las manos (hands)
Nouns ending in consonants	el reloj (watch)	los relojes (watches)
	el papel (role)	los papeles (roles)
	la ciudad (city)	las ciudades (cities)
Nouns ending in -z	el lápiz (pencil)	los lápices (pencils)
	el pez (fish)	los peces (fishes)
	la voz (voice)	las voces (voices)
Nouns ending with -(i)ón	la canción (song)	Las canciones (songs)
	la lección (lesson)	Las lecciones (lessons)
	el avión (plane)	Los aviones (planes)

Nouns for languages and nationalities

- The names of languages in Spanish are masculine with 'el,' and without capital letters unless they are at the start of sentences. For example: el español (Spanish), el francés (French), el inglés (English), el alemán (German), etc.
- Nationality adjectives must agree in gender and number (masc./fem., singular/plural).
  - If it is used for a feminine noun: add **-a**.
  - If it is plural: add **-es** (or **-as** for feminine plural).

Singular	Plural	Gender
El ingles (englishman)	Los ingleses (Englishmen)	Masc.
La inglesa (englishwoman)	Las inglesas (Englishwomen)	Fem.
El español (the spaniard)	Los españoles (Spaniards)	Masc.
La española (the Spanish woman)	Las españolas (Spanish women)	Fem.

Infinitives as nouns (gerund form)

- In Spanish, the infinitive (the basic form of the verb, ending in **-ar**, **-er**, **-ir**) can act as a noun.
- It is often equivalent to English '-ing' words (e.g. correr running).
- For example, he word comer is normally the infinitive of the verb eating but can be used as a noun in a sentence like: el comer es importante (eating is important).
- Examples:
  - El leer es divertido (reading is fun)
  - Viajar es educativo (traveling is educational)
  - El estudiar requiere disciplina (studying requires discipline)

Grammar 1: Nouns, articles, and pronouns

Agreement and definite/indefinite articles

- Articles must match the noun in gender (masculine/feminine) or number (singular/plural).

Definite (the)	Indefinite (a, some)	Gender and number	Example
el	un	Masc. singular	el libro (book)
la	una	Fem. singular	la casa (the house)
los	unos	Masc. plural	los perros (the dogs)
las	unas	Fem. plural	unas chicas (the girls)

- **Definite article:**
  - The definite article 'the' is used for specific nouns. In Spanish, specific ideas often use the definite article (e.g. La educación es importante. (Education is important.)). This is different from English as we wouldn't say '<u>The</u> education is important.'
- **Indefinite articles:** ('a,' 'an,' 'some') are used for non-specific nouns. For example: quiero un coche nuevo. (I want a new car.) Here, the non-specific noun is the car. It is non-specific because it refers to something vague (e.g any car) whereas 'the education' refers to a more specific idea.

Contraction of articles

- When 'de' (meaning 'of' or 'from') is followed by 'el' (the masculine singular definite article), they contract into 'del' (meaning 'of the' or 'from the'). For example:
  - Vengo del cine. (I come from the cinema.) Here, de el becomes del.
  - La llave del coche (The car key). Here, de el becomes del, meaning 'of the car.'
- When 'a' (meaning 'to') is followed by 'el' (the masculine singular definite article), they contract into 'al' (meaning 'to the'). For example:
  - Voy al parque. (I'm going to the park.) Here, a el becomes al.
  - Vamos al trabajo. (We're going to work.) Here, a el becomes al, literally meaning 'to the work.'

Before contraction	After contraction	Meaning
De + el	Del	Of the, from the
A + el	al	To the

Subject pronouns

- **Subject pronouns:** are the words that tell us who is doing the action.

Pronoun	Meaning
yo	I
Tú, tus	you [informal, singular], you [informal, plural]
nosotros / nosotras	we [masc./fem.]
usted (Ud.)	you [formal, singular]
ustedes (Uds.)	you all [formal, plural]
vosotros / vosotras	you all [informal plural]
él	he
ella	she
ellos	they [masc. or mixed]
ellas	they [feminine]

- **Interrogative pronouns:** are used to ask questions about people or things. Some of them change form depending on gender and number.
  - **Cuál / Cuáles (Which? / What?):** changes for number but not gender.
    - ¿Cuál es tu color favorito? (What is your favourite color?)
    - ¿Cuáles son tus libros? (Which are your books?)
  - **Cuánto / Cuánta / Cuántos / Cuántas (How much? / How many?):** changes for gender and number, and must agree with the noun that follows.
    - Cuánto is used for singular masculine nouns – e.g. ¿Cuánto dinero tienes? (How much money do you have?)
    - Cuánta is used for singular feminine nouns – e.g. ¿Cuánta leche queda? (How much milk remains?)
    - Cuántos is used for plural masculine nouns – e.g. ¿Cuántos hermanos tienes? (How many brothers do you have?)
    - Cuántas used for plural feminine nouns – e.g. ¿Cuántas clases hay? (How many classes are there?)
  - **Quién / Quiénes (Who?):** changes for number only (not gender).
    - Quién is used for one noun – e.g. ¿Quién es ella? (Who is she?)
    - Quiénes is used for more than one noun – e.g. ¿Quiénes vienen a la fiesta? (Who is coming to the party?)

Grammar I: Nouns, articles, and pronouns

Object pronouns

- **Direct object pronouns:** are used to replace the thing affected by the verb.

Pronoun	Meaning
me	me
te	you (informal)
lo	him / it (masc.)
la	her / it (fem.)
los	them (masc. or mixed)
las	them (fem.)

  ◦ **One-verb constructions:** the pronoun goes before the verb.
    - **Structure:** [Pronoun] + [Conjugated Verb]
    - Lo veo. *(I see him/it.)*
    - Te escucho. *(I hear you.)*
    - La tengo. *(I have her/it.)*
    - Here, the verbs veo, escucho and tengo are all conjugated verbs. The pronoun must come before these verbs, to indicate that the verb is being done to the pronoun. For example, in the phrase 'lo veo,' veo is a verb that means *I see*, and the 'lo' before it indicates that *I see him/it*.
  ◦ **Two-verb constructions:** come in one of two forms:
    - Option A: pronoun before the first verb.
      ○ Lo quiero mirar. *(I want to look at him/it.)*
    - Option B: Attach the pronoun to the end of the infinitive.
      ○ Quiero mirarlo. *(I want to look at him/it.)*
    In this case, we can either place the pronoun before the two verbs or we attach it to the end of the second verb. Both are correct and mean the same thing.
  ◦ Examples:
    - Necesito comprarlo. / Lo necesito comprar. *(I need to buy it.)*
    - Vamos a invitarla. / La vamos a invitar. *(We're going to invite her.)*
    - Quieren verlo. / Lo quieren ver. *(They want to see him/it.)*
    - Debo terminarla. / La debo terminar. *(I must finish it.)*
    - Puedes llamarme. / Me puedes llamar. *(You can call me.)*

- **Indirect object pronouns:** tell us who is receiving the action of the verb.

Pronoun	Meaning
me	to / for me
te	to / for you (informal)
le	to / for him, her, you (formal)
les	to / for them, you all (formal)

  ◦ For example: Doy el libro a Juan. → Le doy el libro. *(I give the book to Juan → I give the book to him.)*
  ◦ In this example, we can use the indirect object le to indicate that *he* (Juan) is receiving the book. So we can rewrite the sentence: 'I give the book to Juan' as 'I give him the book,' where 'him' replaces 'Juan' and le is the indirect object.
  ◦ To recognise the suitable indirect object (e.g te, le, les...) we can ask who is receiving it. For example, who is receiving the book? In this case it is Juan (i.e. masc. singular) so we must use le.
  ◦ For plurals, the same pattern applies: Escribimos una carta a nuestros padres. → Les escribimos una carta. *(We wrote a letter to our parents. → We wrote a letter to them.)*
  ◦ Examples:
    - Mi mamá me compra una mochila. *(My mom buys a backpack for me.)*
    - Te voy a dar un regalo. / Voy a darte un regalo. *(I'm going to give a gift to you.)*
    - Le contamos la historia. *(We tell the story to her.)*
    - El profesor les explica la tarea. *(The teacher explains the homework to them.)*
    - El camarero le trae el menú. *(The waiter brings the menu to you (formal).)*

- **Affirmative command pronouns:** to form a command from the verb:
  ◦ Remove the -r from -ar verbs.
  ◦ Remove the -r from -er verbs.
  ◦ Remove the -ir from -ir verbs and replace it with -e (e.g. vivir becomes vive).
  ◦ Then, attach the pronoun to the end of the verb.
    - ¡Míralo! *(Look at him/it!)*
    - ¡Cómela! *(Eat it [feminine object]!)*
    - ¡Escúchame! *(Listen to me!)*

Grammar I: Nouns, articles, and pronouns

Possessive pronouns

- Possessive pronouns are words that replace a noun and show who owns something. In English, these are words like: mine, yours, his, hers, ours, theirs. In Spanish, they must agree with both: the thing possessed (its gender and number: masculine/feminine, singular/plural) and the owner (1st, 2nd, 3rd person: I, you, he/she, etc.).

Common Spanish possessive pronouns				
English	Masc. sg.	Fem. sg.	Masc. pl.	Fem. pl.
mine	el mío	la mía	los míos	las mías
yours	el tuyo	la tuya	los tuyos	las tuyas
his/hers/yours	el suyo	la suya	los suyos	las suyas
ours	el nuestro	la nuestra	los nuestros	las nuestras
yours	el vuestro	la vuestra	los vuestros	las vuestras
theirs/yours	el suyo	la suya	los suyos	las suyas

- Examples:
  - **1st person singular:** Este libro es mío. (This book is mine.)
  - **2nd person singular:** Los perros son tuyos. (The dogs are yours.)
  - **3rd person singular:** Los archivos son suyos. (The files are his.)
  - **1st person plural:** La decisión fue nuestra. (The decision was ours.)
  - **2nd person plural:** Las bicicletas son vuestras. (The bikes are yours [pl.].)
  - **3rd person plural:** Las mantas son ellos. (The blankets are theirs.)

Demonstrative and invariable pronouns

- Esto and eso mean *this* and *that* in a general or undefined way. They are used when talking about ideas, situations, or unknown things.
- They are neuter, which means they don't refer to a specific masculine or feminine noun. For example: ¿Qué es esto? (What is this?), ¡Eso es increíble! (That is amazing!), ¿Por qué dijiste eso? (Why did you say that?)
- **Invariable pronouns** refer to unspecified people or things and do not change for gender or number (e.g. algo = *something*, alguien = *someone/somebody*). These pronouns don't agree with verbs or adjectives by gender/number – they're fixed. For example: ¿Oíste algo? (Did you hear something?), Alguien está en la puerta. (Someone is at the door.), ¿Has dicho algo? (Have you said something?)

Reflexive pronouns

- **Singular reflexive pronouns** are used when the **subject and the object are the same person** — the subject does an action **to themselves**.

Pronoun	Meaning
me	*myself*
te	*yourself [informal]*
se	*himself, herself, yourself [formal]*

- **One-verb constructions:** the reflexive pronoun goes **before** the conjugated verb. For example:
  - Me levanto temprano. (I get up early.)
  - Te duchas por la mañana. (You shower in the morning.)
  - Se peina antes de salir. (They comb their hair before going out.)
  - In all these examples, the action is being done to the same person who is doing the action. For example, the first one, has a literal translation of *'I get (myself) up early.'*
- **Plural reflexive pronouns** are used when reflexive verbs use reflexive pronouns (like me, te, se, nos, os) to show that the subject is doing something to themselves (reflexive) or to each other (reciprocal, plural).
  - Reflexive (the subject does something to itself):
    - Nos despertamos a las siete. (We wake ourselves up at 7.)
    - Os acostáis tarde. (You [plural] go to bed late.)
    - Se preparan para el examen. (They prepare themselves for the exam.)
  - Reciprocal (subjects do something to each other):
    - Nos vemos todos los días. (We see each other every day.)
    - Os entendéis muy bien. (You [pl.] understand each other well.)
    - Se besan al saludar. (They kiss each other upon greeting.)

Plural reflexive pronouns		
Person	Reflexive pronoun	Example verb use
nosotros / nosotras	nos	nos saludamos (we greet each other)
vosotros / vosotras	os	os habláis (you [plural] talk to each other)
ellos / ellas / ustedes	se	se ayudan (they help each other)

Grammar II: Verbs

Irregular inflected forms
- Some verbs don't follow regular conjugation patterns – these are called irregular. You need to memorise their unique forms. For example:
    - Dar *(to give)* → Yo doy un regalo. *(I give a gift.)*
    - Decir *(to say)* → Yo digo la verdad. *(I tell the truth.)*
    - Tener *(to have)* → Yo tengo una idea. *(I have an idea.)*
    - Venir *(to come)* → Yo vengo a las cinco. *(I come at five.)*

Present indicative tense
- This is used to express actions that are happening now in the simple present tense (e.g. 'I speak,' 'he eats,' 'they live').

Regular verb endings			
Person	-ar (hablar)	-er (comer)	-ir (vivir)
yo	hablo	como	vivo
tú	hablas	comes	vives
él/ella/usted	habla	come	vive
nosotros/as	hablamos	comemos	vivimos
vosotros/as	habláis	coméis	vivís
ellos/ellas/ustedes	hablan	comen	viven

- It is important to note that the subject pronouns (yo, tu, el, ella, nosotros, vosotros, ellos) can be omitted when writing the present indicative. For example: yo hablo español can be written as hablo español, omitting yo.

Present indicative irregular verb conjugation					
Person	estar *(to be)*	hacer *(to do / to make)*	ir *(to go)*	ser *(to by)*	tener *(to have)*
yo	estoy	hago	voy	soy	tengo
tú	estás	haces	vas	eres	tienes
él/ella/usted	está	hace	va	es	tiene
nosotros/as	estamos	hacemos	vamos	somos	tenemos
vosotros/as	estáis	hacéis	vais	sois	tenéis
ellos/ellas/ustedes	están	hacen	van	son	tienen

- **Estar** *(to be):* used for emotions, location, and temporary conditions.
    - Estoy cansado. *I am tired. (temporary condition)*
    - ¿Estás en casa? *Are you at home? (location)*
    - Ella está feliz. *She is happy. (emotion)*
    - Estamos en clase. *We are in class. (location)*
    - ¿Estáis listos? *Are you all ready? (temporary condition)*
    - Ellos están en el parque. *They are in the park. (location)*
- **Hacer** *(to do / to make):* used for general actions, tasks, and weather.
    - Hago mi tarea. *I do my homework. (tasks)*
    - ¿Haces ejercicio? *Do you exercise? (general actions)*
    - Él hace una pregunta. *He asks a question. (general actions)*
    - Hacemos pan. *We make bread. (general actions)*
    - ¿Hacéis un pastel? *Are you making a cake? (tasks)*
    - Hacen mucho trabajo. *They do a lot of work. (tasks)*
- **Ir** *(to go):* used for locations and directions.
    - Voy al cine. *I go to the cinema.*
    - ¿Vas al supermercado? *Do you go to the supermarket?*
    - Usted va al médico. *You [formal] go to the doctor.*
    - Vamos a la playa. *We go to the beach.*
    - ¿Vais al museo? *Do you all go to the museum?*
    - Ellos van a casa. *They go home.*
- **Ser** *(to be):* used for identity, origin, time, and permanent traits.
    - Soy profesor. *I am a teacher.*
    - Eres muy amable. *You are very kind.*
    - Es ingeniera. *She is an engineer.*
    - Somos hermanos. *We are siblings.*
    - Sois estudiantes. *You all are students.*
    - Son inteligentes. *They are intelligent.*
- **Tener** *(to have):* used in expressions for age and conditions.
    - Tengo sed. *I am thirsty.*
    - ¿Tienes un lápiz? *Do you have a pencil?*
    - Tiene miedo. *He/She is afraid.*
    - Tenemos un perro. *We have a dog.*
    - ¿Tenéis frío? *Are you all cold?*
    - Tienen veinte años. *They are twenty years old.*

Grammar II: Verbs

Present continuous tense
- The present continuous describes what is happening right now (e.g. 'I am eating,' 'she is talking').
- Structure: **estar (in present tense)** + **gerund.**
- To form regular gerunds:
  - -ar verbs → -ando
    e.g. hablar → hablando (speaking)
  - -er / -ir verbs → -iendo
    e.g. comer → comiendo (eating)
- Examples:
  - Using hablar (to speak, regular -ar):
    - Yo estoy hablando. *I am speaking.*
    - Tú estás hablando. *You are speaking.*
    - Él / Ella está hablando. *He/She is speaking.*
    - Nosotros estamos hablando. *We are speaking.*
    - Vosotros estáis hablando. *You all are speaking.*
    - Ellos están hablando. *They are speaking.*
  - Using comer (to eat, regular -er):
    - Estoy comiendo. *I am eating.*
  - Using vivir (to live, regular -ir):
    - Estamos viviendo en Madrid. *We are living in Madrid.*

Special cases of gerunds
- **Spelling change:** this affects verbs whose stem ends in a vowel. For example, the stem of leer is lee-, which ends in a vowel. In these verbs, -yendo is used instead of -iendo. For examples:
  - leer (read) → Estoy leyendo un libro. *(I'm reading a book.)*
  - oír (hear) → Estás oyendo la música. *(You're hearing the music.)*
  - construir (building) → Ellos están construyendo una casa. *(They are building a house.)*
- **Stem-changing -ir verbs (like in the pedir cluster):** some -ir verbs change in the stem and take the -iendo ending. For example:
  - pedir (ask) → Estoy pidiendo ayuda. *(I am asking for help.)*
  - decir (say) → Estás diciendo la verdad. *(You are telling the truth.)*
  - dormir (sleep) → Él está durmiendo. *(He is sleeping.)*
  - servir (serve) → Estamos sirviendo la comida. *(We are serving the food.)*

Present perfect tense
- The present perfect is used to describe actions that have happened recently or that still have relevance to the present (e.g. 'I have walked,' 'she has eaten,' 'we have gone').
- Structure:
  - [Subject] + [conjugated form of haber] + [past participle]
  - The subject can be stated (yo, tú, él, etc.) or implied.
  - The verb haber must agree with the subject (it must be conjugated).
  - The past participle (gerund) stays the same for all subjects
- To form the present perfect:
  - First conjugate haber in the present tense:

Regular verb endings	
Person	haber
yo	he
tú	has
él/ella/usted	ha
nosotros/as	hemos
vosotros/as	habéis
ellos/ellas/ustedes	han

  - Then, add the past participle (or the gerund):
    - For -ar verbs, add -ado (e.g. hablar → hablado *spoken*).
    - For -er/-ir verbs, add -ido (e.g. comer → comido *eaten*).
- Examples with regular verbs:
  - Yo he hablado con ella. *(I have spoken with her.)*
  - Tú has comido pizza. *(You have eaten pizza.)*
  - Él ha vivido en España. *(He has lived in Spain.)*
  - Nosotros hemos trabajado mucho. *(We have worked a lot.)*
  - Vosotros habéis estudiado bien. *(You all have studied well.)*
  - Ellos han leído el libro. *(They have read the book.)*

Grammar II: Verbs

Preterite tense (simple past)

- The preterite tense is used for the simple past tense (e.g. I saw, you drank, they left).

Regular preterite verb conjugation			
Person	hablar (to speak)	comer (to eat)	vivir (to live)
yo	hablé	comí	viví
tú	hablaste	comiste	viviste
él/ella/usted	habló	comió	vivió
nosotros/as	hablamos	comimos	vivimos
vosotros/as	hablasteis	comisteis	vivisteis
ellos/ellas/ustedes	hablaron	comieron	vivieron

- Examples:
  - Ir (to go) → Fuimos al museo ayer. (We went to the museum yesterday.)
  - Ser (to be) → La fiesta fue divertida. (The party was fun.)
  - Dar (to give) → Le di el dinero al camarero. (I gave the money to the waiter.)
  - Tener (to have) → Ayer tuve una reunión importante. (I had an important meeting yesterday.)
  - Estar (to be) → El sábado estuvimos en Madrid. (On Saturday we were in Madrid.)
  - Poder (can) → No pude abrir la puerta. (I couldn't open the door.)
  - Poner (to put) → Ella puso el libro sobre la mesa. (She put the book on the table.)
  - Saber (to find out) → Supimos la verdad ayer. (We found out the truth yesterday.)
  - Hacer (to do / make) → ¿Qué hiciste anoche? (What did you do last night?)
  - Querer (to want / try) → Quise ayudarte, pero fue tarde. (I tried to help you, but it was late.)
  - Venir (to come) → Mis amigos vinieron a la fiesta. (My friends came to the party.)
  - Decir (to say / tell) → Te dije la verdad. (I told you the truth.)
  - Traer (to bring) → ¿Tú trajiste el vino? (Did you bring the wine?)
  - Ver (to see) → Vi una película excelente. (I saw an excellent movie.)

- Some verbs have **irregular preterite forms** that you just need to memorise. Ir and ser share the same forms, but the others are different.

Irregular preterite verb conjugation													
Person	ir (went)	ser (was)	dar (gave)	tener (had)	estar (was)	poder (could)	poner (put)	saber (knew)	hacer (did)	querer (wanted)	venir (came)	decir (said)	traer (brought)	venir (saw)
yo	fui		di	tuve	estuve	pude	puse	supe	hice	quise	vine	dije	traje	vi
tú	fuiste		diste	tuviste	estuviste	pudiste	pusiste	supieste	hiceste	quisiste	viniste	dijiste	trajiste	viste
él/ella/usted	fue		dio	tuvo	estuvo	pudo	puso	supo	hizo	quiso	vino	dijo	trajo	vio
nosotros/as	fuimos		dimos	tuvimos	estuvimos	pudimos	pusimos	supimos	hicimos	quisimos	vinimos	dijimos	trajimos	vimos
vosotros/as	fuistes		disteis	tuvisteis	estuvisteis	pudisteis	pusisteis	supisteis	hicisteis	quisisteis	vinisteis	dijisteis	trajisteis	visteis
ellos/ellas/ustedes	fueron		dieron	tuvieron	estuvieron	pudieron	pusieron	supieron	hicieron	quisieron	vinieron	dijeron	trajeron	vieron

Grammar II: Verbs

Irregular past participles

- Some high frequency verbs don't follow the -ado/-ido pattern.

Infinitive	Irregular past participle/gerund
abrir	abierto *(opened)*
decir	dicho *(said)*
escribir	escrito *(written)*
hacer	hecho *(done/made)*
poner	puesto *(put)*
ver	visto *(seen)*
volver	vuelto *(returned)*
morir	muerto *(died)*
romper	roto *(broken)*
cubrir	cubierto *(covered)*

- Note: prefixes (like des- or re-) apply but aren't listed separately in the vocabulary list if the base verb is listed. For example, descrito = *described* (from escrito), resuelto = *resolved* (from vuelto).
- Examples with irregular past participles:
  - (Yo) He escrito una carta. *(I have written a letter.)*
  - ¿(Tu) Has dicho la verdad? *(Have you told the truth?)*
  - Ella ha abierto la ventana. *(She has opened the window.)*
  - (Nosotros) Hemos hecho la tarea. *(We have done the homework.)*
  - (Ellos) Han visto esa película. *(They have seen that movie.)*

Imperfect past continuous tense

- The imperfect continuous is used to describe actions that were ongoing or in the past. It is more common in spoken Spanish.
- Structure: [Estar in imperfect] + [present participle (gerund)]
- Examples:
  - Yo estaba estudiando. *(I was studying.)*
  - Tú estabas leyendo un libro. *(You were reading a book.)*
  - Él estaba comiendo. *(He was eating.)*
  - Nosotros estábamos jugando al fútbol. *(We were playing football.)*
  - Ellos estaban viendo una película. *(They were watching a movie.)*

Imperfect tense

- The imperfect tense in Spanish describes one of two scenarios:
  - Habitual past actions (what someone used to do)
  - Ongoing or background actions in the past (was/were + -ing in English – e.g 'you were speaking')

Regular imperfect conjugation			
Person	hablar (to speak)	comer (to eat)	vivir (to live)
yo	hablaba	comía	vivía
tú	hablabas	comías	vivías
él / ella / usted	hablaba	comía	vivía
nosotros/as	hablábamos	comíamos	vivíamos
vosotros/as	hablabais	comíais	vivíais
ellos / ellas / ustedes	hablaban	comían	vivían

- Yo hablaba con ella cuando él entró.
  (I was talking to her when he walked in.) [ongoing action]
- Tú hablabas mucho cuando eras niño.
  (You used to talk a lot when you were a child.) [habitual]
- Ella comía cuando sonó el teléfono.
  (She was eating when the phone rang.) [ongoing]
- Nosotros comíamos pizza todos los viernes.
  (We used to eat pizza every Friday.) [habitual]
- Yo vivía en Madrid en ese momento.
  (I was living in Madrid at that time.) [ongoing]
- Ellos vivían cerca del mar cuando eran niños.
  (They used to live near the sea when they were kids.) [habitual]

Irregular imperfect conjugation			
Person	ser (to be)	ir (to go)	ver (to see)
yo	era	iba	veía
tú	eras	ibas	veías
él / ella / usted	era	iba	veía
nosotros/as	éramos	íbamos	veíamos
vosotros/as	erais	ibais	veíais
ellos / ellas / ustedes	eran	iban	veían

Grammar II: Verbs

Periphrastic future tense

- The periphrastic future is used to talk about actions that are going to happen soon (e.g. 'I am going to eat,' 'We are going to travel').
- Structure: [ir (conjugated)] + a + [infinitive verb]

Subject	ir (to go) [present tense]
yo	voy
tú	vas
él / ella / usted	va
nosotros/as	vamos
vosotros/as	vais
ellos / ellas / ustedes	van

- Examples with vivir:
  - Yo voy a vivir en España. *(I'm going to live in Spain.)*
  - Tú vas a vivir aquí. *(You are going to live here.)*
  - Ella va a vivir con nosotros. *(She is going to live with us.)*
  - Nosotros vamos a vivir juntos. *(We are going to live together.)*
  - Vosotros vais a vivir en Madrid. *(You all are going to live in Madrid.)*
  - Ellos van a vivir bien. *(They are going to live well.)*

Inflectional future tense

- The inflectional future tense is used to express what will happen in the future. It's equivalent to "will + verb" in English (e.g. 'I will study').
- Structure: for -ar, -er, and -ir verbs, the same set of endings is added to the full infinitive of the verb (not just the stem).

Regular inflectional future conjugation			
Person	hablar (to speak)	comer (to eat)	vivir (to live)
yo	hablaré	comeré	viviré
tú	hablarás	comerás	vivirás
él / ella / usted	hablará	comerá	vivirá
nosotros/as	hablaremos	comeremos	viviremos
vosotros/as	hablaréis	comeréis	viviréis
ellos / ellas / ustedes	hablarán	comerán	vivirán

- Examples:
  - Hablaré con ella mañana. *(I will talk to her tomorrow.)*
  - Comerás en casa esta noche. *(You will eat at home tonight.)*
  - Vivirán en México el próximo año. *(They will live in Mexico next year.)*
  - Estudiaremos para el examen. *(We will study for the exam.)*
  - Trabajará en una oficina nueva. *(He/she will work in a new office.)*

- **Irregular verb future tense formation:** these verbs are irregular only in the stem (tendr-, podr-, har-, pondr-), but the endings are regular for future tense.

Future tense for irregular verbs					
Person	saber (to know)	querer (to want)	venir (to come)	decir (to say)	salir (to leave)
yo	sabré	querré	vendré	diré	saldré
tú	sabrás	querrás	vendrás	dirás	saldrás
él / ella / usted	sabrá	querrá	vendrá	dirá	saldrá
nosotros/as	sabremos	querremos	vendremos	diremos	saldremos
vosotros/as	sabréis	querréis	vendréis	diréis	saldréis
ellos / ellas / ustedes	sabrán	querrán	vendrán	dirán	saldrán

- Examples:
  - Yo tendré mucho trabajo mañana. *(I will have a lot of work tomorrow.)*
  - Ella tendrá una entrevista importante. *(She will have an important interview.)*
  - Tú podrás venir con nosotros. *(You will be able to come with us.)*
  - Usted podrá ver los resultados mañana. *(You will be able to see the results tomorrow.)*
  - Yo haré mi presentación pronto. *(I will do my presentation soon.)*
  - Tú harás una gran diferencia. *(You will make a big difference.)*
  - Yo pondré los libros en la mesa. *(I will put the books on the table.)*
  - Él pondrá atención en clase. *(He will pay attention in class.)*

Grammar II: Verbs

Conditional tense

- The conditional tense is equivalent to the English 'would + verb' construction (e.g. 'I would cook dinner but I'm too tired'). In Spanish, it is used to express one of three scenarios:
  - What would happen under certain conditions (e.g. Comerías más si te gustara la comida. *You would eat more if you liked the food.*)
  - Polite requests (e.g. ¿Hablarías un poco más despacio, por favor? *Would you speak a little more slowly, please?*)
  - Hypotheticals (e.g. Hablaría con ella, pero no sé dónde está. *I would talk to her, but I don't know where she is.*)

Conditional tense conjugation					
Person	tener (to have)	haber (to have)	hacer (to do)	poder (can)	poner (to put)
yo	tendría	habría	haría	podría	pondría
tú	tendrías	habrías	harías	podrías	pondrías
él / ella / usted	tendría	habría	haría	podría	pondría
nosotros/as	tendríamos	habríamos	haríamos	podríamos	pondríamos
vosotros/as	tendríais	habríais	haríais	podríais	pondríais
ellos / ellas / ustedes	tendrían	habrían	harían	podrían	pondrían

- Yo tendría más tiempo si no trabajara tanto. (*I would have more time if I didn't work so much.*)
- ¿Tú tendrías paciencia en esa situación? (*Would you have patience in that situation?*)
- Ella haría un pastel si tuviera los ingredientes. (*She would make a cake if she had the ingredients.*)
- ¿Qué harías tú en mi lugar? (*What would you do in my place?*)
- Yo podría ayudarte mañana. (*I could help you tomorrow.*)
- Ellos podrían ganar si tuvieran más dinero. (*They could win if they had more money.*)
- Él pondría el libro en la biblioteca. (*He would put the book in the library.*)
- ¿Dónde pondrías tú la mesa? (*Where would you put the table?*)
- Habría más gente si el clima fuera mejor. (*There would be more people if the weather were better.*)
- No habría problema en cambiar la hora. (*There would be no problem changing the time.*)

Affirmative commands

- The affirmative tú command is used to give commands.
- For regular verbs, the command form is the 3rd person singular of the present indicative. In Spanish, you use this when speaking to:
  - One person (tú) [informal]
  - A group of people (vosotros/as) [informal]

Verb type	Infinitive	Tú (you)	Vosotros/as (you all)
-ar	hablar	habla	hablad
-er	comer	come	comed
-ir	vivir	vive	vivid

- ¡Habla más despacio! (*Speak more slowly!*)
- ¡Habla con tu profesor! (*Talk to your teacher!*)
- ¡Come tus verduras! (*Eat your vegetables!*)
- ¡Vive tu vida con alegría! (*Live your life with joy!*)
- ¡Vive el momento! (*Live the moment!*)

Irregular affirmative 'tú' commands		
Infinitive	Affirmative tú command	Meaning
ser	sé	*be*
ir	ve	*go*
tener	ten	*have*
venir	ven	*come*
hacer	haz	*do / make*
decir	di	*say / tell*
poner	pon	*put / place*
salir	sal	*leave / go out*

- ¡Sé valiente! (*Be brave!*)
- ¡Ve a casa! (*Go home!*)
- ¡Ten cuidado! (*Be careful! / Have caution!*)
- ¡Ven aquí! (*Come here!*)
- ¡Haz la tarea! (*Do the homework!*)
- ¡Di la verdad! (*Tell the truth!*)
- ¡Pon la mesa! (*Set the table!*)
- ¡Sal de la habitación! (*Leave the room!*)

Grammar II: Verbs

Subjunctive mood

- The subjunctive mood is used in Spanish when we talk about: wishes, hopes, requests, emotions, commands, doubt, uncertainty, or things that might happen in the future, especially after cuando *(when)*, or to show purpose with para que *(so that)*.
- You usually see it after the word que.

Person	Subjunctive mood conjugation				
	tener (to have)	hacer (to do)	venir (to come)	ser (to be)	ir (to go)
yo	tenga	haga	venga	sea	vaya
tú	tengas	hagas	vengas	seas	vayas
él / ella / usted	tenga	haga	venga	sea	vaya

- **After cuando to talk about the future:** when you're referring to something that hasn't happened yet, use the subjunctive.
    - Cuando venga, hablaremos. *(When he comes, we'll talk.)*
    - Cuando tengas tiempo, llámame. *(When you have time, call me.)*
- **After verbs of wishing, command, request, or emotion:** when one person wants or feels something about another person's action.
    - Quiero que hagas la tarea. *(I want you to do the homework.)*
    - Espero que vayas al médico. *(I hope you go to the doctor.)*
    - Me alegra que seas tan amable. *(I'm happy that you are so kind.)*
- **After que in general:** when one part of a sentence shows an opinion, and it's followed by que, the verb after que is in the subjunctive.
    - Es importante que tengas cuidado. *(It's important that you be careful.)*
- **After para que *(so that)*:** used to show purpose.
    - Te explico esto para que lo entiendas. *(I'm explaining this so that you understand it.)*

Interesar-type verbs

- Verbs like interesar *(to interest)*, gustar *(to like)*, encantar *(to love)*, and doler *(to hurt)* follow a different sentence structure than most English sentences. Instead of saying '*I like chocolate*,' in Spanish we would say: Me gusta el chocolate. The literal translation of this would be 'To me pleases chocolate' (Indirect Object + Verb [3rd person] + Subject).
- Common indirect object pronouns:
    - gustar *(to like)*
    - encantar *(to love)*
    - interesar *(to interest)*
    - doler *(to hurt)*
    - molestar *(to bother)*
    - fascinar *(to fascinate)*
    - importar *(to matter)*
    - parecer *(to seem / appear)*
    - quedar *(to remain / be left)*
    - faltar *(to lack / be missing)*

English	Spanish
to me	me
to you	te
to him/her	le
to us	nos
to you all	os
to them	les

- Examples:
    - Me interesa la historia. *(History interests me.)* Literally: "To me interests history"
    - ¿Te gusta la música clásica? *(Do you like classical music?)* Literally: "Does classical music please you?"
    - Le encanta el cine. *(He/she loves the cinema.)* Literally: "To him loves the cinema"
    - Nos duele la cabeza. *(We have a headache.)* Literally: "To us hurts the head."

Impersonal verbs

- **Use of the impersonal verb hay *(there is / there are)*:** never changes form for singular or plural. For example: Hay un libro en la mesa. *(There is a book on the table.)* or Hay muchas personas aquí. *(There are many people here.)*
- **Use of hay que + infinitive *(one must / it is necessary to)*:** this is used in general cases, i.e. not referring to a specific person. For example: Hay que estudiar para el examen. *(One must study for the exam.)* or Hay que limpiar la casa. *(It's necessary to clean the house.)*
- **Impersonal use of se (for generalised *you / one*):** this use of se makes a sentence impersonal, meaning it applies to people in general. This is often translated as *'you can,' 'one needs to,'* etc. For example: Se puede nadar aquí. *(You/One can swim here.)*, Se necesita tiempo. *(Time is needed.)*, or Se come bien en este restaurante. *(One eats well in this restaurant.)*
- **Use of hace + noun (for weather):** hace is used for certain weather expressions, and always stays the same, e.g. Hace frío. *(It's cold.)*.

Grammar II: Verbs

Modal verbs

- Modal verbs are special verbs that help you express **ability, obligation, desire,** or **knowledge** (e.g. can, must, have to, want, etc.).
- They are always followed by another verb in its basic form (infinitive), like: estudiar *(to study)*, comer *(to eat)*, salir *(to leave)*, etc.
- Structure: [Person] + [modal verb – conjugated] + [infinitive verb]
- Note: The indication of person e.g yo, el, ella, ellos, etc. is optional.
- Example: (Yo) debo estudiar. *(I must study.)*

Modal verb	Meaning
deber	should / must
poder	can / to be able to
querer	to want
tener que	to have to
saber	to know how to
quisiera	I would like (to)
(me/te/le/les/os) gustaría	(I/you/he or she or you formal/ they all) would like (to)

- Examples:
  - Yo debo estudiar para el examen. *(I must study for the exam.)*
  - Debes beber agua. *(You should drink water.)*
  - Yo puedo hablar. *(I can speak.)*
  - ¿Puedes venir mañana? *(Can you come tomorrow?)*
  - Quiero comer. *(I want to eat.)*
  - ¿Tu quieres salir conmigo? *(Do you want to go out with me?)*
  - Tengo que trabajar hoy. *(I have to work today.)*
  - Tienes que hacer la tarea. *(You have to do the homework.)*
  - Sé nadar muy bien. *(I know how to swim very well.)*
  - ¿Sabes tocar la guitarra? *(Do you know how to play the guitar?)*
  - Quisiera reservar una mesa. *(I would like to reserve a table.)*
  - Me gustaría viajar a México. *(I would like to travel to Mexico.)*
  - ¿Te gustaría ir al cine? *(Would you like to go to the cinema?)*

Reflexive verbs

- Reflexive verbs are actions that a person does to themselves.
- In Spanish, they use special words called reflexive pronouns: me, te, se (for 1st, 2nd, 3rd person singular). These show that the subject does something to itself. Reflexive pronouns come before the reflexive verb.
- You can tell if a verb is reflexive if it ends in -se in the infinitive, e.g. lavarse *(to wash oneself)*, vestirse *(to dress oneself)*.
- Examples:
  - Yo me lavo. *(I wash myself)*
  - Tú te lavas. *(You wash yourself)*
  - Él se lava. *(He washes himself)*
- Compare this to the non-reflexive version:
  - Yo lavo el coche. *(I wash the car.)* [not reflexive]
- Some verbs change their meaning when reflexive:

Base verb	Reflexive form	Meaning change
poner	ponerse	to become / to put on (clothes)
dormir	dormirse	to fall asleep (not just sleep)
sentar	sentarse	to sit down (yourself)

Reflexive verb conjugation			
Person	lavarser (-ar) (to wash)	comerse (-er) (to eat)	vestirse (ir, stem-changing) (to get dressed)
yo	me lavo	me como	me visto
tú	te lavas	te comes	te vistes
él / ella / usted	se lava	se come	se viste
nosotros/as	nos lavamos	nos comemos	nos vestimos
vosotros/as	os laváis	os coméis	os vestís
ellos / ellas / ustedes	se lavan	se comen	se visten

Grammar III: Adjectives and adverbs

Positions of adjectives

- In Spanish, the default position for adjectives is after the noun. For example:
  - un coche rojo (a red car)
  - una casa grande (a big house)
  - un perro feliz (a happy dog)
- However, some adjectives come before the noun – these are called **prenominal adjectives.** These are often short, common adjectives.

Premonimal adjective	Meaning	Example
algún	some / any	¿Tienes algún libro? (Do you have any book?)
ningún	no / none	No tengo ningún amigo. (I don't have any friend.)
primer	first	Es el primer día. (It's the first day.)
segundo	second	Mi segundo intento. (My second try.)
tercer	third	El tercer capítulo. (The third chapter.)
buen	good	Es un buen estudiante. (He's a good student.)
mal	bad	Tuviste un mal día. (You had a bad day.)
gran	great	Es una gran idea. (It's a great idea.)

- Some adjectives change meaning depending on their position

Adjective	Before noun (prenominal)	After noun (postnominal)
único	only	unique
antiguo	former	old
pobre	unfortunate	poor (without money)
gran	great	big (grande)

- Examples:
  - Mi único amigo (my only friend) vs. Un amigo único (a unique friend)
  - Mi antigua casa (my former house) vs. Una casa antigua (an old house)
  - Un pobre hombre (an unfortunate man) vs. Un hombre pobre (a poor man)

Gender and number agreement of adjectives

- Adjectives must agree with the gender (masculine/feminine) and number (singular/plural) of the noun they describe. For example:
  - **-o = masculine singular:** El chico guapo (The handsome boy)
  - **-a = feminine singular:** La chica guapa (The pretty girl)
  - **-os = masculine plural:** Los chicos guapos (The handsome boys)
  - **-as = feminine plural:** Las chicas guapas (The pretty girls)
- Some adjectives don't change for gender but do for number.
  - **-e/-es:** same for masculine/feminine; add -s for plural:
    - El chico inteligente (The intelligent boy)
    - La chica inteligente (The intelligent girl)
    - Los chicos inteligentes (The intelligent boys)
    - Las chicas inteligentes (The intelligent girls)
  - **-z:** change to -ces for plurals:
    - Un chico feliz (A happy boy)
    - Dos chicos felices (Two happy boys)
    - Una niña feliz (A happy girl)
    - Unas niñas felices (some happy girls)
  - **-ista/-istas:** no change for gender; add -s for plurals:
    - El estudiante futbolista (the footballer student)
    - La estudiante futbolista (the footballer student)
    - Los estudiantes futbolistas (the footballer students)
    - Las estudiantes futbolistas (the footballer students)
- Adjectives of nationality have specific spelling patterns.
  - Adjectives ending in consonants usually follow the pattern: **-és, -esa, -eses, -esas**. Note that the accent on -és disappears in plural. For example:
    - El chico francés (The French boy)
    - La chica francesa (The French girl)
    - Los chicos franceses (The French boys)
    - Las chicas francesas (The French girls)
  - Another pattern: **-ol, -ola, -oles, -olas**. For example:
    - El chico español (The Spanish boy)
    - La chica española (The Spanish girl)
    - Los chicos españoles (The Spanish boys)
    - Las chicas españolas (The Spanish girls)

Grammar III: Adjectives and adverbs

Comparative adjectives

- The regular comparative structure of **menos... que** is used to say that something is less than something else.
- Structure: **[subject] + verb + menos + [adjective/adverb/noun] + que + [comparison]**
- Examples:
  - Este coche es menos rápido que el otro. *(This car is less fast than the other one.)*
  - Yo tengo menos tiempo que tú. *(I have less time than you.)*
  - Ella estudia menos que su hermana. *(She studies less than her sister.)*
- There are also some irregular comparatives used instead of más bueno and más malo.

Irregular comparatives		
Word	Meaning	Used instead of
mejor	better	más bueno
peor	worse	más malo

- Examples:
  - Esta película es mejor que la anterior.
    (This movie is better than the previous one.)
  - Su comportamiento fue peor que ayer.
    (His behaviour was worse than yesterday.)

Demonstrative adjectives

- These adjectives point out or demonstrate a specific noun. They agree with the gender and number of the noun they modify. For example, in the phrase este libro *(this book)*, este is masculine and singular which agrees with the masculine singular noun libro.

Singular	Plural
Este libro *(this book, masc.)*	Estos libros *(these, masc.)*
Esta casa *(this house, fem.)*	Estas casas *(these, fem.)*
Ese auto *(that car, masc.)*	Esos autos *(those cars, masc.)*
Esa chica *(that, feminine)*	Esas chicas *(those girls, fem.)*

Indefinite adjectives

- Indefinite adjectives describe nouns in a non-specific way. In Spanish, they can express ideas like 'each,' 'same,' 'other,' 'all,' or 'some.'
- It is non-specific because it doesn't point to a specific thing. For example: Algún libro es interesante *(some book is interesting)*. Here, algún *(some)* doesn't refer to a specific item.
- Many agree in gender and number but some are invariable meaning they do not change at all. The list below specifies which adjectives agree with nouns or are invariable.
  - **cada** *(each, every):* – invariable; only with singular nouns.
    - Cada estudiante tiene un libro. *(Each student has a book.)*
    - Voy al gimnasio cada día. *(I go to the gym every day.)*
  - **mismo** *(same):* agrees in gender and number of the noun.
    - El mismo problema otra vez *(The same problem again)*
    - Las mismas ideas que ayer *(The same ideas as yesterday)*
  - **otro** *(other, another):* agrees with the gender and number of the noun.
    - Quiero otro café. *(I want another coffee.)*
    - Compré otras camisas. *(I bought other shirts.)*
  - **todo** *(all, every):* agrees with gender and number of the noun.
    - Todo el mundo está aquí. *(Everyone is here.)*
    - Todas las casas son blancas. *(All the houses are white.)*
  - **alguno / algún** *(some, any):* algún is used before a singular masculine noun, whereas alguno changes form to match gender and number (alguna, algunos, algunas).
    - ¿Tienes algún libro interesante? *(Do you have any interesting books?)*
    - Algunos amigos vendrán. *(Some friends will come.)*
  - **ninguno / ningún** *(none, not any):* ninguno (changes to ninguna for feminine) is typically used in singular form, whereas ningún is used before a singular masculine noun.
    - No tengo ningún lápiz. *(I don't have any pencil.)*
    - Ninguna respuesta fue correcta. *(No answer was correct.)*

Grammar III: Adjectives and adverbs

Possessive adjectives

- Possessive adjectives show ownership or relationship, just like in English (e.g. my, your, his, her, our, etc.).
- In Spanish, they must agree with the noun in number (and sometimes gender).
  - **Mi / Mis** *(my):*
    - Mi casa es grande. *(My house is big.)*
    - Mis amigos son simpáticos. *(My friends are nice.)*
  - **Tu / Tus** *(your – informal singular):*
    - Tu perro es bonito. *(Your dog is cute.)*
    - Tus libros están aquí. *(Your books are here.)*
  - **Su / Sus** *(his, her, its, their, your – formal):*
    - Su coche es nuevo. *(His/her/their/your (formal) car is new.)*
    - Sus ideas son buenas. *(His/her/their/your(formal) ideas are good.)*
    - In this case, there is only an agreement for the number; it is genderless.
    - Sus is used for plural and su is used for singular.
  - **Nuestro / Nuestra / Nuestros / Nuestras** *(our):*
    - Nuestro profesor es inteligente. *(Our teacher is smart.)* Here, nuestro is masculine and singular and agrees with the equally masculine and singular profesor.
    - Nuestras mochilas están aquí. *(Our backpacks are here.)* Here, nuestras is feminine and plural and agrees with the feminine and plural mochilas.
  - **Vuestro / Vuestra / Vuestros / Vuestras** *(your – plural informal):*
    - Again in these two examples, there is format agreement, just like the examples given for nuestro.
    - Vuestra casa es bonita. *(Your [plural informal] house is pretty.)* Here the format is: feminine singular
    - Vuestros hijos son altos. *(Your kids are tall.)* Here the format is: masculine plural

Position of adverbs

- Adverbs and adverbial phrases give more information about:
  - When something happens (time)
  - How it happens (manner)
  - Where it happens (place)
- Adverbs of time are usually at the beginning or end of the sentence. For example:
  - Hoy vamos al parque. *(Today we're going to the park.)*
  - Vamos al parque mañana. *(We're going to the park tomorrow.)*
- Adverbs of manner are usually placed after the verb. For example:
  - Habla rápidamente. *(He/She speaks quickly.)*
  - Trabajan bien juntos. *(They work well together.)*
- Adverbs of place often come after the verb. For example:
  - Está aquí. *(He/She is here.)*
  - Caminamos al parque. *(We walked to the park.)*

Comparative structures with adverbs

- We use comparative adverbs to compare how, when, or where things happen.

Structure	Meaning	Example
más... que	more... than	Ella corre más rápido que su hermano. *(She runs faster than her brother.)*
menos... que	less... than	Juan trabaja menos que Pedro. *(Juan works less than Pedro.)*
tan... como	as... as	Marta habla tan claro como Ana. *(Marta speaks as clearly as Ana.)*

- For numbers, use más/menos de + number. For example:
  - Tengo más de cinco libros. *(I have more than five books.)*
  - Hay menos de diez personas. *(There are fewer than ten people.)*
- Some adverbs have irregular forms:

Base form	Comparative	Meaning	Example
bien	mejor	better	Ella canta mejor que yo. *(She sings better than I do.)*
mal	peor	worse	Él juega peor que su primo. *(He plays worse than his cousin.)*

Grammar IV: Prepositions and other grammar functions

Types of prepositions

- Prepositions are short words used before nouns or infinitives to show direction, place, time, cause, possession, etc.
- **Personal a:** when the direct object of a verb is a person or pet, Spanish uses the personal a before it. This has no direct translation in English.
    - Veo a mi madre. *(I see my mother.)*
    - Busco a Juan. *(I'm looking for Juan.)*
    - Escucho a mi perro. *(I listen to my dog.)*
- **De to indicate possession:** use de to express that something belongs to someone. It works like the possessive ('s) in English.
    - Es la casa de Hugo. *(It's Hugo's house.)*
    - El libro de María. *(María's book.)*
    - La opinión del profesor. *(The teacher's opinion.)*
- **Para, sin + infinitive:** some prepositions are followed directly by an infinitive verb (the base form).
    - Estudio para sacar buenas notas. *(I study in order to get good grades.)*
    - Salió sin decir nada. *(He left without saying anything.)*
- **Verb + preposition combinations:** some verbs must be followed by a specific preposition when used with another verb or noun. These are called fixed expressions, and the preposition can change or add to the verb's meaning. Here are a few common examples:

Verb phrase	Meaning	Example
dejar de + infinitive	to stop doing something	Dejé de fumar. *(I stopped smoking.)*
ir de + noun	to go (on/for)	Fuimos de compras. *(We went shopping.)*
llegar a + infinitive	to manage to do something	Llegué a entenderlo. *(I managed to understand it.)*
soñar con + noun/infinitive	to dream of/about	Sueño con viajar. *(I dream of traveling.)*
pensar en + noun/infinitive	to think about	Pienso en ti. *(I think about you.)*

Preposition suffixes

- **Suffix -ito/-ita:** added to nouns to express either smallness (e.g. like the English 'little') or affection/endearment (e.g like 'dear' or 'cute'). This is formed by adding -ito to masc. nouns, and -ita to fem. nouns. Sometimes, the final vowel -o or -a is dropped before adding the suffix. For example: perro → perrito *(little dog / doggie)*, casa → casita *(little house / cottage)*, hermano → hermanito *(little brother / dear brother)*.
- **Suffix -ísimo/-ísima:** added to adjectives to intensify their meaning (like 'very' in English). This is formed by adding -ísimo to masc. adjectives, adding -ísima to fem. adjectives, and removing the final -o/-a before adding the suffix, e.g. fácil → facilísimo *(very easy)*, bonita → bonitísima *(very pretty)*.

Suffix patterns

- In Spanish, just like in English, we can change words a bit to create new words. We do this by adding little parts to the end of a word – these are called suffixes. These patterns help us turn:
    - **Adjectives into adverbs with -mente** (like *slow → slowly*)
        - If the adjective ends in -o, change it to -a first. Then just add -mente. For example:
        - rápido → rápidamente *(quickly)*
        - lento → lentamente *(slowly)*
        - normal → normalmente *(normally)*
        - fácil → fácilmente *(easily)*
        - alegre → alegremente *(happily)*
    - **Adjectives into nouns with -idad** (like *happy → happiness*)
        - Add -idad to an adjective to make it a noun. For example:
        - real → realidad *(reality)*
        - curioso → curiosidad *(curiosity)*
        - feliz → felicidad *(happiness)*
        - seguro → seguridad *(safety/security)*
        - necesario → necesidad *(necessity)*
    - **Verbs into adjectives with -able** (like *believe → believable*)
        - Spanish does the same as English! Just add -able or -ible to the verb. For example:
        - evitar → evitable *(avoidable)*
        - comprender → comprensible *(understandable)*
        - creer → creíble *(believable)*
        - acceder → accesible *(accessible)*

Grammar IV: Prepositions and other grammar functions

Negation

- In Spanish, to make a sentence negative, you usually place 'no' before the verb:
- Structure: no + verb + rest of sentence
- Common negative words:
  - no (not)
  - nada (nothing / anything)
  - nunca (never)
  - nadie (no one / nobody)
  - ninguno(a) (none / not any)
- Examples:
  - No como carne. (I don't eat meat.)
  - No tengo nada. (I have nothing / I don't have anything.)
  - No viene nadie. (No one is coming.)
  - No veo nunca a Juan. (I never see Juan.)
  - No tengo ninguno. (I don't have any / I have none.)
- Other negation phrases include:
  - ya no (no longer / not anymore): used before the verb to express that something used to happen but doesn't anymore.
    - Ya no vivo allí. (I no longer live there.)
    - Ya no estudia medicina. (He/she doesn't study medicine anymore.)
  - **(no) tampoco (neither / not ... either):** used to agree in the negative with a previous statement, usually placed before the verb in negative form.
    - No me gusta el café. — A mí tampoco. (I don't like coffee. — Me neither.)
    - Ella no quiere salir, y yo tampoco. (She doesn't want to go out, and neither do I.)
  - **(no)...ni... (not...nor...):** used to negate two or more elements. The no is optional but adds clarity or emphasis.
    - No tengo ni dinero ni tiempo. (I don't have money or time.)
    - No llamó ni escribió. (He/she neither called nor wrote.)
  - **(no) ni...ni... (emphatic negation):** this form stresses that none of the mentioned elements apply.
    - Ni come ni duerme. (He/she neither eats nor sleeps.)
    - Ni tú ni yo sabemos la respuesta. (Neither you nor I know the answer.)

Subject relative clauses and 'que'

- First we must explain what is the subject relative clause. This is a part of a sentence that tells us **more about a person or thing**, and the **person or thing is doing something** in that extra part. For example:
  - El hombre que vive en Madrid es mi profesor. (The man who lives in Madrid is my teacher.)
  - Here the subject clause would be 'que vive en madrid' because its the part of the sentence that tells us more about the man, and it tells us that the man is living in Madrid.
- Therefore, in a subject relative clause, we use 'que' to replace the subject (person or thing) of the second part of the sentence and link it to the main noun we're talking about. Therefore, que is the person or thing doing the action in the second part. It's used to join two ideas into one sentence and avoid repeating the subject. For example:
  - El niño que corre es mi hermano. (The boy who runs is my brother.)
  - La película que gana premios es muy buena. (The movie that wins awards is very good.)
  - Los chicos que juegan aquí son mis amigos. (The boys who play here are my friends.)
  - Tengo un perro que ladra mucho. (I have a dog that barks a lot.)

Questions

- You can ask yes/no questions using normal word order and raising your voice at the end. This is called upwards intonation. For example:
  - Tú comes carne. (You eat meat.)
  - ¿Tú comes carne? (Do you eat meat?)
- Spanish also has special question words (wh-words), like: Qué (what), Quién (who), Cuándo (when), Por qué (why), Cómo (how), Cuál (which), Cuánto/a/os/as (how much/many), and Dónde (where).
- The word order for questions with 'wh' words is: wh-word + verb + subject (the subject is optional but can be placed after the verb for clarity). For example:
  - ¿Dónde está Daniel? (Where is Daniel?)
  - ¿Qué hace la chica? (What is the girl doing?)
  - ¿Cómo estás? (How are you?) [the subject is understood as tú]
  - ¿Quién viene? (Who is coming?) [the subject is quién itself]
  - ¿Cuándo vamos al cine? (When are we going to the movies?)

Grammar IV: Prepositions and other grammar functions

Spelling changes in verb stems

- Some Spanish verbs change their spelling in certain forms to keep the original sound consistent with pronunciation rules. These spelling changes usually occur in the first person singular (yo) or the third person singular/plural in the preterite tense, present, or other forms where the spelling affects pronunciation.
- Examples:
  - escoger → yo escojo
  - buscar → yo busqué
  - empezar → yo empecé
  - llegar → yo llegué
  - leer → él leyó, ellos leyeron
- Some Spanish -ir verbs (like dormir, pedir, preferir) change a little bit in the past tense (preterite), but only in the third person (he/she/they). These small changes happen in the middle of the word (the stem) – it's like a vowel swap where 'o' becomes 'u' and 'e' becomes 'i'. For example:
  - **Dormir** *(to sleep)* → **change 'o' to 'u'**
    - Yo dormí *(I slept)*
    - Tú dormiste *(You slept)*
    - El/ella/usted durmió *(He/she/you (formal) slept)*
    - Ellos durmieron *(They slept)*
  - **Pedir** *(to ask for)* → **change 'e' to 'i'**
    - Yo pedí *(I asked.)*
    - Tú pediste. *(You asked)*
    - El/ella/usted pidió *(He/she/you (formal) asked)*
    - Ellos pidieron *(They asked)*
  - **Preferir** *(to prefer)* → **change 'e' to 'i'**
    - Yo preferí *(I preferred)*
    - Tú preferiste *(You preferred)*
    - El/ella/usted prefirió *(He/she/you (formal) preferred)*
    - Ellos prefirieron *(They preferred)*

Multi verb expressions

- **Acabar de** + **infinitive**: used to say someone has just done something (very recently).
  - Structure: acabar (present tense) + de + infinitive
    - Yo acabo de comer. *(I have just eaten.)*
    - Ella acaba de llegar. *(She has just arrived.)*
- **Passive voice:** there are two ways to express passive voice in Spanish.
  - a) **Ser + past participle + por:** this structure is used to say something was done by someone, focusing on the action and the person who did it. It's called the passive voice. It's called the passive voice because the subject of the sentence is "passive" – it receives the action instead of doing it. For example the active sentence 'García Márquez wrote the book' becomes 'The book was written by García Márquez.'
    - Structure: ser (in any tense) + past participle + por + agent
      - El libro fue escrito por García Márquez. *(The book was written by García Márquez.)*
      - La casa será construida por mi padre. *(The house will be built by my father.)*
  - b) **Se + 3rd person verb:** we use this to say that people in general do something without saying exactly who.
    - Structure: se + 3rd person verb (conjugated for he, she, it, they)
      - Se vende pan aquí. *(Bread is sold here.)*
      - Se hacen pasteles. *(Cakes are made.)*
- **Seguir + present participle:** to say someone is still doing something.
  - Structure: seguir (present) + present participle (-ando/-iendo)
    - Sigo estudiando español. *(I'm still studying Spanish.)*
    - Él sigue trabajando. *(He's still working.)*
- **Llevar + time period + present participle:** used to say how long someone has been doing something (like: "I have been doing this for 2 years.")
  - Structure: llevar (present) + time period + present participle (-ando/-iendo)
    - Llevo dos años estudiando español. *(I've been studying Spanish for two years.)*
    - Lleva media hora esperando. *(He/She has been waiting for half an hour.)*
- **Present tense + desde hace + time:** another way to say how long someone has been doing something.
  - Structure: present tense verb + desde hace + time period
    - Vivo aquí desde hace cinco años. *(I've lived here for five years.)*
    - Trabaja en esa empresa desde hace un mes. *(He/she has been working there for a month.)*

Reading skills

General advice

- Typically, reading sections in tests and exams will have something like the following structure:
  - Section A: Answer in English - based on short Spanish texts
  - Section B: Answer in Spanish - based on longer and more complex Spanish texts
  - Section C: Translate a passage from Spanish to English
- The extracts and texts will normally include lots of additional details but the questions will require you to focus on a specific detail. Make sure that you are able to pull out the specific detail being questioned by looking for key words in the extract, e.g if being asked about where a person lives, look for the keyword vivo (I live) or any other conjugated form of vivir (to live).
- Solid knowledge of specific vocabulary related to each of the themes is crucial, but if it arises that you are unsure of any word, you can guess the vague meaning from its context. For example:
  - Es una ciudad tranquila gracias a las zonas peatonales. Tener aparcamientos en las afueras es bueno. Hacen falta caminos para bicicletas.
  - Suppose that for this extract we are unsure of the word caminos. From its context, we can see that it is something to do with bicycles and city infrastructure because it mentions bicicletas and zonas peatonales (pedestrian zones). We also know that there is something lacking for it because it says hacen falta (they are needed). Based on this information, we can speculate that the unknown word is something that is missing for bicycles, like a bicycle path, station/parking etc.
  - If we already know the words that refer to some of the ideas, like aparcamiento (parking), we are able to make a more educated guess that caminos means path.
- Always have in mind that the texts often include words that you haven't studied before. The exam knows this and it is trying to test your ability to understand unfamiliar words from the context around them.
- Watch out for negatives: words such as tampoco may seem like they are affirming some given information when they are actually negating it. For example, tampoco soy fan de futbol (I am not a football fan either).
- Recognise and use **cognates**. These are words that look and sound similar to their English translation e.g hospital, animal, importante. But also be careful of **false friends** like embarazada which means pregnant, not embarrassed.

High-frequency vocabulary for reading tasks

These are key words that come up again and again:
- **Time phrases:**
  - ayer (yesterday)
  - hoy (today)
  - mañana (tomorrow)
  - el año pasado (last year)
  - en el futuro (in the future)
- **Question words:**
  - quién (who)
  - qué (what)
  - cuándo (when)
  - dónde (where)
  - por qué (why)
  - cómo (how)
  - cuánto (how much)
- **Connectives:**
  - porque (because)
  - pero (but)
  - sin embargo (however)
  - además (also)
  - aunque (although)
- **Quantifiers:**
  - mucho (a lot)
  - poco (a little)
  - bastante (enough)
  - demasiado (too much)
  - nada (none)
- **Common verbs:**
  - ser (to be, for permanent things like identity, origin)
  - estar (to be, for temporary things like location, emotion)
  - tener (to have, posession)
  - haber (is / are, auxilliary verb)
  - ir (to go)
  - hacer (to do / to make)
  - gustar (to like)
  - querer (to want / to love)

Reading skills

Tips for answering in English
- Read the text first then the question, then once more look at the text to find the answer. This makes it faster to find the relevant information.
- Underline keywords in the question (wh- words like why, when, where) as well as any other essential words.
- For example: in the question *Why does Marta say she prefers living in the countryside rather than the city?* you may want to highlight or underline the words shown.
- Be **concise** but accurate in your English answers – don't make up or assume information not found in the text
- If being asked about whether an opinion is positive or negative look for negative or positive word qualifiers.
- Here are some of the most common qualifiers:
  - **Positive opinion qualifiers:**
    - me gusta / me encanta / me chifla *(I like / I love)*
    - es genial / estupendo / fantástico / maravilloso *(it's great / fantastic / wonderful)*
    - es útil / interesante / importante *(it's useful / interesting / important)*
    - disfruto (de) *(I enjoy)*
    - prefiero / me fascina / me interesa *(I prefer / I'm fascinated by / I'm interested in)*
    - lo paso bien / me lo paso bomba *(I have a good time / I have a blast)*
  - **Negative opinion qualifiers:**
    - odio / detesto / no me gusta / me molesta *(I hate / I can't stand / I don't like / it annoys me)*
    - es aburrido / terrible / horrible *(it's boring / terrible / awful)*
    - es una pérdida de tiempo *(it's a waste of time)*
    - me fastidia / me irrita / me da asco *(it annoys me / it irritates me / it disgusts me)*
    - lo paso mal / me aburre *(I have a bad time / it bores me)*

Tips for answering in Spanish
- When answering, you can use words from the text where possible, but don't just copy long sentences - try to formulate your response.
- Write in simple Spanish – clarity and accuracy is much more important than complexity.
- Learn to express opinions in Spanish using phrases like ella piensa que, el hombre opina que, yo creo que, etc.
- Pay attention to tenses and make sure to match the tense used in the question if needed. For example:
  - **Question:** ¿Qué hizo Marta el fin de semana pasado?
  - **Answer:** El fin de semana pasado Marta fue al cine con sus amigos.

Tips for translating texts
- Read and re-read the whole text multiple times to **grasp the meaning.**
- Break the text into smaller chunks and translate clause by clause. For example, in this Spanish sentence: 'Aunque hacía frío, salimos al parque porque queríamos jugar al fútbol.' there are **3 clauses**:
  - aunque hacía frío *(Although it was cold)*
  - salimos al parque *(we went out to the park)*
  - porque queríamos jugar al fútbol *(because we wanted to play football)*
- The aim is to translate into natural English, not word-for-word translations. For example, if we have the following sentence in Spanish: 'Ayer por la tarde, mi hermana y yo fuimos al centro comercial porque necesitábamos comprar ropa para el invierno.' the literal translation would be something like: *'Yesterday for the afternoon, my sister and I went to the centre commercial because we needed to buy clothes for the winter.'* But the more natural translation would be: *'Yesterday afternoon, my sister and I went to the shopping centre because we needed to buy winter clothes.'*
- If you don't recognise a Spanish word, always try to infer its meaning from the context.
- Don't worry too much about getting every word perfect – aim for overall sense.
- If stuck on any part of the text that you don't understand, leave a gap and come back later.

Writing skills

General advice
- Make sure to understand and highlight the key words of each question to see what exactly is expected from you.
- Pay special attention to the expected format of the piece. If it says escribele un email a tu amigo Juan, it means that it is expecting a written piece in the format of an email. In that case you must use appropriate email style openings and sign offs, e.g Hola Juan, espero que estes bien (Hi Juan, I hope that you are well) then when signing off, write atentamente (sincerely).
- In addition to being obligated to respond to all of the bullet points, you must address each with the expected tense e.g if the bullet point says qué hiciste la última vez que fuiste al centro de la ciudad you are expected to form the past tense correctly to talk about something you did at the city centre the last time you visited there.
- Make sure to give both negative and positive opinions, using negative and positive qualifiers.
- When asked about your opinion about something, make sure to justify it with the correct phrases e.g Me gusta escuchar a musica pop dado que/porque/ya que es muy guay.
- Plan before you write. Take 2-3 minutes to write notes for each bullet point and tense.
- Include some higher tier structures/phrases to boost your marks, such as:
  - Suelo + infinitive (I usually...)
  - Acabo de + infinitive (I have just...)
  - Si tuviera más tiempo + conditional (If i had more time...)
  - Me habría gustado + infinitive (I would have liked...)
- Leave at least 3-5 minutes to proofread. Make sure to check for gender/noun agreements, spelling, and proper tense formation.

Tips for short-answer questions
- You need to address all bullet points given in the question (usually 4), so **aim for around 20-25 words** for each one. This avoids writing under or over the recommended word count.
- Use a range of **past, present, and future** tenses. Some of the bullet points may already address any of the tenses, make sure to include the other remaining tenses.
  - For example the question may ask you to menciona (mention):
    - qué hiciste recientemente para mantenerte en forma
    - si prefieres pasar tiempo con muchos amigos o con un amigo especial
    - tu opinión sobre el Internet
    - qué vas a hacer en el futuro para ayudar a otras personas.
  - The first bullet point addresses the past tense, the last one addresses the future tense. Therefore you can write something in the present tense whilst addressing the second or third bullet points.
- You can learn fixed structures that you can adapt quickly to form the tenses (e.g El año pasado fui a..., En el futuro me gustaria...).

Tips for long-response questions
- These questions require **more development and variety** in comparison to the previous questions. There may also be less scaffolding with suggested bullet points or things you need to mention, meaning you need to be able to brainstorm and structure your own answer.
- For these questions, as well as including the 3 tenses (past, present, and future) we can use the conditional tense (e.g me gustaria beber cafe).
- Just like before, makes sure to include two opinions and two justifications.
- You can use paragraphs to structure clearly (e.g. one paragraph for each bullet point, if given). It is advisable to write a short introduction paragraph e.g one or two lines.

Tips for translation into Spanish
- Some questions will require you to translate an English text into natural Spanish. Remember that this is **not** meant to be a word-for-word literal translation. For example:
  - For the English text: '*I went to the beach with my family last summer. We swam in the sea, ate ice cream, and watched the sunset. It was an amazing day.*'
  - The literal translation would be: 'Yo fui a la playa con mi familia el último verano. Nosotros nadamos en el mar, comimos helado, y miramos el sol bajarse. Fue un día asombroso.'
  - But, the more natural translation would be: 'Fui a la playa con mi familia el verano pasado. Nadamos en el mar, comimos helado y vimos la puesta de sol. Fue un día increíble.'
- The examiners are looking for three things: accurate grammar, natural translation, and appropriate vocabulary.
- If unsure of a word, use a synonym or rephrase.

Listening and speaking skills

General advice

- Before the recording starts, you will usually have approximately five minutes to read through the paper. It is crucial that you use these five minutes to underline key words in the questions (e.g when, why, opinion, activity, adjective). After this, start predicting possible answers in your head.
- If you miss anything, don't panic – you will hear everything twice, so don't give up if you miss it the first time. Focus on trying to understand the overall meaning and any keywords – there will be lots of filler or unknown words that are just distractors.
- The speaker may mention multiple different options before finally giving the correct one. For example: Pensé en ir al cine, pero al final fui al parque. The speaker mentions going to cinema, but actually ended up going to the park instead.
- Use the pause between recordings to prepare for what's coming or for making your mind up for the previous question. Make sure to scan the rubrics and underline any key words.
- Listen out for synonyms; the examiners love to use synonyms to trick you (e.g deberes instead of tarea).
- Write numbers as you hear them and generally any other type of answer
- **For answering in English:**
  - Focus on overall meaning – knowing the exact Spanish phrases isn't necessary.
  - If you hear a list, be attentive – the correct answer might come last.
- **For answering in Spanish:**
  - The written answers must have the correct grammar and spelling
  - Use words directly from the recording if possible. That's the safest option and it avoids making up your own ideas.
  - Always try to stick to short, specific answers.

Tips role play tasks

- For these assessments, you are usually given one minute to prepare, so use that time to understand each bullet point and translate it into Spanish. Identify who you are speaking to and where you are.
- You must cover all bullet points, aim for one sentence at least for each. And if the time runs out, say at least something for each bullet point.
- Make sure to cover all the tenses in your answers: present for the current facts, past for what happened, and future to say what you will do.
- Pay attention to the expected register; if it's a friend you must address them with tu, and if it's a teacher you must address them with usted.
- Occasionally add extra details, by adding one extra piece of information (e.g además, también).
- Practise common scenarios like:
  - Booking accommodation
  - Ordering food
  - Asking for direction
  - Making complaints
  - Arranging transport
- If you make any mistakes, just self correct and move on.
- On your paper, try not to write whole answers as this will cost you time and will sound very scripted upon delivery of speech. Rather, try to write some brief ideas in Spanish where you can expand on that when being asked.
- For the unexpected question, don't rush into the answer. Let the question settle in first and after having thought about what to say, you can start to speak. You can ask the examiner to repeat the question as many times as you like – you won't be penalised.
- You are also expected to ask a question about a given bullet point. Think of a short and focused question and write it down on your preparation sheet. You are not expected to ask any follow up questions after that.

Speaking skills

General advice

- Practise speaking your answers out loud regularly. You can then record yourself and check for the following: pronunciation, fluency and use of opinions and correct tenses.
- Aim to show four key skills in every answer: **opinions**, **justifications**, **tenses**, and **connectives**.
- For example: En el futuro me gustaría viajar a México porque me encanta la cultura.
  (In the future I would like to travel to Mexico because I love the culture.)
- If you forget a word, you can rephrase it or describe it. Examiners look for communication, not perfection. For example if you forgot the word for cinema (cine) you could say el lugar donde la gente ven peliculas (the place where people see the movies). This is much better than staying silent or panicking because you can't recall a specific word.
- Memorising certain common structures makes it much easier to formulate your thoughts and ideas more fluently at the exam. You could use structures like:
  - Yo pienso que... (I think that...)
  - Me parece que... (it seems to me that...)
  - Suelo + infinitive (I tend to do something)
  - La razón es que... (the reason is that...)
  - Acabo de + infinitive... (I have just)
  - En mi opinión... (In my opinion)
- Try to speak slowly and clearly – clarity of speech is more important than rushing to cram in lots of vocabulary.

Tips for photo description tasks

- For these tasks you will also have approximately one minute of prep time in which you can use to plan 2–3 sentences for describing the photo. In that time, you can also predict possible questions.
- Start with the basics:
  - Describe **who** is in the photo: personas (hombre, mujer, niños, amigos...)
  - Describe **where** they are: lugar (playa, cocina, parque, colegio...)
  - Mention **what** they're doing: acción principal (hablando, comiendo, jugando...)
- Use timed tenses:
  - **Present** to describe what you see – e.g. En la foto veo a una familia que celebra un cumpleaños.
    (In the photo I see a family celebrating a birthday)
  - **Imperfect preterite** to give context or ongoing actions – e.g. Antes, los niños jugaban en el jardín.
    (Before, children played in the garden.)
  - **Future** to speculate what will happen next – e.g. Después, van a comer tarta y cantar felicitaciones.
    (Afterwards, they will eat cake and sing congratulations.)
  - **Conditional** for formal situations – e.g. Probablemente necesitarían limpiar el desastre más tarde.
    (They would probably need to clean up the mess later.)
- Add details:
  - Clothes and their colors – e.g. Llevan camisetas rojas y vaqueros azules. (They wear red t-shirts and blue jeans.)
  - Emotions and expressions – e.g. Se les ve felices y sonrientes. (They look happy and smiling.)
  - Objects – e.g. Hay globos y una tarta en la mesa. (There are balloons and a cake on the table.)
- Integrate varied vocabulary:
  - Use vocabulary from the themes (e.g. fiesta, comida, tiempo libre, escuela)
  - Employ adjectives and adverbs (e.g. alegre, divertido, cuidadosamente, rápidamente)
  - Include words of perception (e.g. parecer, se ve)
- Opina y justifica:
  - Form a simple opinion – e.g. Me parece una celebración divertida. (I think it's a fun celebration.)
  - Justify that opinion with a reason – e.g. porque todos están sonriendo y compartiendo comida.
    (because everyone is smiling and sharing food.)
- Make comparisons: use words like más... que, menos... que, tan... como – e.g. Este regalo es más grande que el anterior. (This gift is bigger than the last one.)
- Time management: you can mentally organise your time into three blocks:
  1. Objective description (quién, dónde, qué)
  2. Opinion and justification
  3. Compare with your own experience
  - You must speak for a total of 90 seconds, so don't spend too much time in one block.
- Use discursive markers to join ideas (e.g. además, por otro lado, sin embargo, finalmente). This can also help you avoid long pauses while you think!

Theme vocabulary: personal life

Family and relationships

el abuelo = *grandfather*
la abuela = *grandmother*
el adolescente / adolescente = *adolescent*
amigo = *friend*
amistad = *friendship*
amar = *to love*
el anciano / anciano = *(very) old / old person*
el bebé = *baby*
boda = *wedding*
caer bien / mal = *to like / dislike someone*
casado = *married*
el casamiento = *wedding*
casarse = *to get married*
compromiso = *engagement*
comprometerse = *to get engaged*
confiar = *to trust*
cuidar / ocuparse de = *to take care of*
discutir = *to argue / to discuss*
divorciarse = *to get divorced*
enamorarse = *to fall in love*
esposo = *husband*
estado civil = *marital status*
el hermanastro = *stepbrother*
el hijo (único) = *(only) child*
los hijos = *children*
huérfano = *orphan*
la madrastra = *stepmother*
el marido = *husband*
el matrimonio = *marriage, married couple*
el miembro = *member*
la mujer = *woman / wife*
el nieto = *grandchild*
el niño = *child*
noviazgo = *courtship / relationship*
novio / novia = *boy/girlfriend / fiancé / fiancée*
el padrastro = *stepfather*
la pareja = *partner*
los parientes = *relatives*
el primo = *cousin*
el tío = *uncle*
viudo = *widower*

Life stages and time

la adolescencia = *adolescence*
el adulto = *adult*
el anciano = *elderly person*
el cumpleaños = *birthday*
cumplir años = *to have a birthday*
la edad = *age*
la infancia = *childhood*
el joven = *young person*
joven = *young*
la juventud = *youth / young people*
jubilarse = *to retire*
jubilado = *retired*
el jubilado = *pensioner*
la madurez = *maturity / middle age*
la muerte = *death*
nacer = *to be born*
nacido = *born*
el nacimiento = *birth*
la niñez = *infancy / early childhood*
la tercera edad = *senior years*
la vejez = *old age*

Feelings and emotions

aburrido = *bored*
abrazar = *to hug*
agradecido = *grateful*
alegre = *cheerful / happy*
alivio = *relief*
amor = *love*
amigable = *friendly*
angustia = *distress / anguish*
animado = *lively / animated*
ansioso = *anxious*
apenado = *sorry / regretful*
asustado = *scared / frightened*
avergonzado = *embarrassed / ashamed*
cansado = *tired*
celoso = *jealous*
confiado = *confident / trusting*

Personality and appearance

alegre = *happy*
alto = *tall*
amable = *kind*
amistoso = *friendly*
animado = *lively*
antipático = *unfriendly*
el aspecto = *appearance, looks*
bajo = *short*
la barba = *beard*
el bigote = *moustache*
calvo = *bald*
la cara = *face*
cariñoso = *affectionate, tender*
castaño = *chestnut, brown*
comprensivo = *understanding*
débil = *weak*
egoísta = *selfish*
extrovertido = *outgoing*
feo = *ugly*

confundido = *confused*
contento = *glad / happy*
curioso = *curious*
decepcionado = *disappointed*
deprimido = *depressed*
desesperado = *desperate*
dolido = *hurt (emotionally)*
echar de menos = *to miss someone*
emocionado = *excited / moved*
enamorarse = *to fall in love*
enfadado = *angry / annoyed*
enojado = *angry*
entusiasmado = *enthusiastic*
estresado = *stressed*
estar enamorado = *to be in love*
felicidad = *happiness*
feliz = *happy*
fastidiar = *to annoy / to bother*

fuerte = *strong*
las gafas = *glasses*
guapo = *good-looking*
honrado = *honest*
joven = *young-looking*
liso = *straight (hair)*
moreno = *dark(-haired, -skinned)*
orgulloso = *proud*
parecerse a = *to look like*
pelirrojo = *red-haired*
perezosa = *lazy*
rizado = *curly*
rubio = *blonde*
seguro de sí mismo = *self-assured*
serio = *serious, responsible*
simpático = *kind, nice, pleasant*
tímido = *shy*
torpe = *clumsy*
travieso = *naughty, mischievous*
valiente = *brave, bold*
vejo = *old-looking*

frustrado = *frustrated*
furioso = *furious*
herido = *hurt / wounded*
inseguro = *insecure*
llorar = *to cry*
molestar = *to bother*
nervioso = *nervous*
orgulloso = *proud*
preocupado = *worried*
relajado = *relaxed*
satisfecho = *satisfied*
sentimiento = *feeling*
solo = *alone*
solitario = *lonely*
sorprendido = *surprised*
tener ganas de = *to feel like*
tranquilo = *calm / relaxed*
triste = *sad*

Dialogue examples: personal life

Family and relationships

A: ¿Cómo es tu familia?
(What is your family like?)
B: Vivo con mi madre, mi padrastro y mi hermanastro. También tengo una abuela que vive cerca.
(I live with my mom, my step-dad and my step-sister. I also have a grandmother that lives nearby.)

A: ¿Tienes primos?
(Do you have any cousins?)
B: Sí, tengo tres primos. Uno de ellos se llama Pablo. Es simpático y muy divertido.
(Yes, I have three cousins. One of them is named Pablo. He's nice and very funny.)

A: ¿Vas a ir al casamiento de tu prima?
(Are you going to your cousin's wedding?)
B: Sí, se casa el sábado. Estoy muy emocionado porque me encanta ver a toda la familia reunida.
(Yes, she is getting married this Saturday. I am very excited because I love to see the whole family together.)

A: ¿Confías en tu pareja?
(Do you trust your partner?)
B: Sí, tenemos mucha confianza y nos tratamos con respeto.
(Yes, we trust each other a lot and treat each other with respect.)

Personality and appearance

A: ¿Cómo eres físicamente?
(What are you like physically?)
B: Soy bastante alto, tengo el pelo castaño y los ojos verdes. Llevo gafas también.
(I am quite tall, I have brown hair and green eyes. I also wear glasses.)

A: ¿Cómo es tu mejor amiga?
(What is your best friend like?)
B: Es amable y simpática. Siempre me ayuda con los deberes.
(She is friendly and nice. She always helps me with my homework.)

A: Tu hermano se parece a ti?
(Does your brother look like you?)
B: Solo un poco. Él tiene el pelo rizado y moreno, pero yo tengo el pelo liso y rubio. Él heredó su físico de nuestro padre, mientras que yo me parezco más a nuestra madre. Sin embargo, los dos tenemos ojos verdes
(Only a bit. He has brown and curly hair, but I have straight and blonde hair. He inherited his looks from our father whereas I look more like our mother. However, we both have green eyes.)

Life stages and time

A: ¿Cuántos años tienes? (How old are you?)
B: Tengo quince. Voy a cumplir dieciséis el mes que viene. (I am 15. I'm going to be 16 next month.)
A: ¡Qué bien! ¿Vas a hacer algo especial? (How great! Are you going to do something special?)
B: Sí, voy a tener una fiesta con mis amigos. (Yes, I'm going to have a party with my friends.)

A: ¿Eres el más joven de tu familia? (Are you the youngest of your family?)
B: No, mi hermana es más joven. Yo nací en 2009 y ella en 2012.
(No, my sister is the youngest. I was born in 2009 and her in 2012.)
A: ¿Y tus abuelos? (And your grandparents?)
B: Están jubilados y viven en el campo. (They are retired and live in the countryside.)

A: ¿Cuándo es tu cumpleaños? (When is your birthday?)
B: Es el cinco de abril. ¡Tengo muchas ganas de celebrarlo! (It's the fifth of April. I look forward to celebrating it!)
A: ¿Qué planes tienes? (What plans do you have?)
B: Voy a salir a cenar con mi familia. (I'm going to go out to dine with my family.)

A: ¿Dónde naciste? (Where were you born?)
B: Nací en Madrid, pero me mudé a Valencia cuando nació mi hermano.
(I was born in Madrid, but I moved to Valencia when my brother was born.)
A: ¿Recuerdas algo del nacimiento de tu hermano? (Do you remember something from the birth of your brother?)
B: Sí, yo tenía ocho años. Fue un momento muy especial. (Yes, I was eight years old. It was a special moment.)

Feelings and emotions

A: ¿Que pasa? Pareces enfadado.
(What happened? You seem angry?)
B: Sí, mi hermano me molesta todo el tiempo y me fastidia cuando uso su ordenador.
(Yes, my brother annoys me all the time and annoys me when I use his computer.)

A: ¿Estás enamorado de alguien?
(Are you in love with someone?)
B: Sí, me enamoré de una chica de mi clase. Es simpática y muy divertida.
(Yes, I fell in love with a girl from my class. She is sympathetic and very fun.)

A: ¿Qué sentiste en tu cumpleaños?
(How did you feel on your birthday?)
B: Sentí mucha felicidad. Toda mi familia estaba allí y fue un día muy especial.
(I felt a lot of happiness. All of my family were there and it was a very special day.)

Theme vocabulary: leisure activities

Leisure and free time

la actividad = *activity*
bailar = *to dance*
cantar = *to sing*
cocinar = *to cook*
coleccionar = *to collect*
el concierto = *concert*
creativo = *creative*
el deporte = *sport*
deportivo = *sporty*
dibujar = *to draw*
escuchar música = *to listen to music*
la excursión = *excursion / trip*
la fiesta = *party*
el juego = *game*
leer = *to read*
montar en bicicleta = *to ride a bike*
el ocio = *leisure / free time*
la película = *film / movie*
el paseo = *outing / stroll*
pasear = *to go for a walk*
practicar deporte = *to do sport*
la reunión = *meeting / get-together*
la salida = *outing*
la sala de fiestas = *dance hall / nightclub*
salir = *to go out*
el tiempo libre = *free time*
ver la tele = *to watch TV*

Entertainment and media

la actuación = *performance / acting*
el actor = *actor*
la actriz = *actress*
la cadena = *TV channel*
la cámara = *camera*
El canal de YouTube = *YouTube channel*
el concurso = *quiz show / competition*
El creador de contenido = *content creator*
el directo / la transmisión en vivo = *live stream*
el documental = *documentary*
los dibujos animados = *cartoons*
el escenario = *stage*
el espectáculo = *show / performance*
la estrella = *star*
la entrevista = *interview*
la fotografía = *photography*
la gira = *tour*
el guion = *script*
la historia = *story*
el juego = *game / fun / amusement*
los Juegos Olímpicos = *Olympic Games*
las noticias = *news*
la obra de teatro = *play (theatre)*
la opinión = *opinion / review*
el papel = *role*
la película = *film / movie*
la prensa = *the press*
la publicidad = *advertising*
la radio = *radio*
la red = *the internet / the web*
la red social = *social media*
la revista = *magazine*
el sequidor = *follower*
la serie = *series (TV)*
la suscripción = *subscription*
la telenovela = *soap opera*
la televisión = *television*
la transmisión en directo = *live broadcast*
el vídeo = *video*
el videojuego en línea = *online video game*
la viralidad = *virality*

Sports and physical activities

el atleta = *athlete*
el baloncesto = *basketball*
el béisbol = *baseball*
el boxeo = *boxing*
el campo = *field / pitch*
el ciclismo = *cycling*
correr = *to run*
el deporte = *sport*
el ejercicio = *exercise*
el esquí = *skiing*
el fútbol = *football / soccer*
el gimnasio = *gym*
el jugador = *player*
jugar = *to play*
levantar pesas = *to lift weights*
la lucha libre = *wrestling*
la natación / nadar = *swimming / to swim*
el partido = *match / game*
el patinaje = *skating*
la pista = *track / court / run / slope / rink*
el rugby = *rugby*
el senderismo = *hiking*
el surf = *surfing*
el tenis = *tennis*
el torneo = *tournament*
el voleibol = *volleyball*

Music and performance

los altavoces = *speakers*
la armonía = *harmony*
los auriculares = *headphones*
la balada = *ballad*
la banda / el grupo = *band / group*
el bajo = *bass*
la batería = *drums / drum kit*
el compás = *beat / time signature*
el concierto = *concert*
el compositor / la compositora = *composer*
el coro = *choir / chorus*
el director de orquesta = *conductor*
el disco = *record / album*
el ensayo = *rehearsal*
la escala = *scale*
la flauta = *flute*
el flamenco = *flamenco*
la guitarra = *guitar*
el jazz = *jazz*
la letra = *lyrics*
la melodía = *melody*
el micrófono = *microphone*
la música = *music*
la música clásica = *classical music*
la nota = *note*
la ópera = *opera*
el órgano = *organ*
el piano = *piano*
el pop = *pop*
el público = *audience*
la canción = *song*
la grabación = *recording*
el ritmo = *rhythm*
el rock = *rock*
el saxofón = *saxophone*
el escenario = *stage*
el solista = *soloist*
la sinfonía = *symphony*
el tambor = *drum*
tocar = *to play (an instrument)*
el tono = *tone / key*
la trompeta = *trumpet*
el violín = *violin*
la voz = *voice*

Dialogue examples: leisure activities

Leisure and free time

A: ¿Qué haces normalmente en tu tiempo libre?
(What do you usually do in your free time?)
B: Me gusta salir con mis amigos y dar un paseo por el parque.
(I like going out with my friends and taking a walk in the park.)

A: Este sábado vamos a una sala de fiestas. ¿Quieres venir?
(This Saturday we're going to a club. Do you want to come?)
B: ¡Claro! Me encantan las salidas con música y baile.
(Of course! I love outings with music and dancing.)

A: Ayer tuve una reunión con mis antiguos compañeros de clase.
(Yesterday I had a reunion with my old classmates.)
B: ¡Qué bien! ¿Dónde fue la reunión? (That's great! Where was the reunion?)
A: En una cafetería en el centro. (At a café in the city centre.)

A: ¿Fuiste a la fiesta de Ana anoche? (Did you go to Ana's party last night?)
B: Sí, estuvo genial. Bailamos, reímos y comimos mucha pizza.
(Yes, it was great. We danced, laughed, and ate lots of pizza.)

A: En mi tiempo libre practico muchos deportes. (In my free time I do a lot of sports.)
B: ¿Eres muy deportivo entonces? (So you're very sporty then?)
A: Sí, juego al fútbol y nado dos veces por semana. (Yes, I play football and swim twice a week.)

A: ¿Te apetece pasear esta tarde? (Do you feel like going for a walk this afternoon?)
B: Sí, me encanta dar paseos al atardecer. (Yes, I love taking walks at sunset.)

A: No tengo tiempo libre esta semana. (I don't have any free time this week.)
B: ¡Qué pena! El ocio es importante para descansar.
(That's a shame! Leisure time is important to relax.)

Music and performance

A: ¿Tocas algún instrumento musical? (Do you play a musical instrument?)
B: Sí, toco el piano desde hace tres años. (Yes, I've played the piano for three years.)

A: ¿Te gusta escribir letras de canciones? (Do you like writing song lyrics?)
B: Sí, cuando estoy inspirado escribo letras sobre mis emociones.
(Yes, when I'm inspired I write lyrics about my emotions.)

A: ¿Alguna vez has estado en un concierto de música? (Have you ever been to a music concert?)
B: Sí, vi a Taylor Swift de gira el año pasado. Al público le encantó su actuación.
(Yes, I saw Taylor Swift on tour last year. The audience loved her performance.)

Entertainment and media

A: ¿Te gustó la película de ayer? (Did you like yesterday's film?)
B: Sí, la historia era emocionante y el papel del protagonista fue increíble.
(Yes, the story was exciting and the main character's role was incredible.)

A: ¿Has visto el nuevo documental sobre animales marinos?
(Have you seen the new documentary about sea animals?)
B: Sí, me encantó. Aprendí mucho y las imágenes eran preciosas.
(Yes, I loved it. I learned a lot and the visuals were beautiful.)

A: ¿Qué tipo de programas te gustan? (What kind of programmes do you like?)
B: Las telenovelas no me interesan, pero me gustan los espectáculos en directo.
(I'm not into soap operas, but I like live shows.)

A: ¿Veías dibujos animados de pequeño? (Did you watch cartoons as a child?)
B: Sí, me encantaba uno con una estrella mágica que salvaba el mundo.
(Yes, I loved one with a magic star that saved the world.)

Sports and physical activities

A: ¿Ganasteis el partido? (Did you win the match?)
B: Sí, marqué un gol en los últimos minutos. ¡Fue increíble!
(Yes, I scored a goal in the last few minutes. It was amazing!)

A: ¿Qué haces los sábados? (What do you do on Saturdays?)
B: Juego al baloncesto por la mañana y después voy a nadar.
(I play basketball in the morning and then I go swimming.)

A: ¿Sabes patinar bien? (Can you skate well?)
B: Más o menos. Practico en la pista de hielo cada viernes.
(More or less. I practise at the ice rink every Friday.)

A: ¿Has ido de pesca alguna vez? (Have you ever gone fishing?)
B: Sí, fui con mi padre el verano pasado. Me gusta pescar, es muy relajante.
(Yes, I went with my dad last summer. I like fishing, it's very relaxing.)

A: ¿Participaste en el torneo de tenis? (Did you take part in the tennis tournament?)
B: No este año, pero sí el año pasado. Fue una gran experiencia.
(Not this year, but I did last year. It was a great experience.)

A: ¿Montas en bici a menudo? (Do you ride your bike often?)
B: Sí, me encanta montar por la montaña con mis amigos.
(Yes, I love riding in the mountains with my friends.)

A: ¿Has probado el monopatín alguna vez? (Have you ever tried skateboarding?)
B: Sí, pero me caí muchas veces. No soy muy bueno todavía.
(Yes, but I fell a lot. I'm not very good yet.)

Theme vocabulary: daily life and travel

Home

- el armario = wardrobe
- arreglar = to tidy / to fix
- el aseo = bathroom / WC
- el ascensor = lift / elevator
- la alfombra = carpet / rug
- alquilado = rented
- alquilar = to rent / to hire
- el aparcamiento = parking
- el baño = bathroom / bath
- el barrio = neighbourhood
- la calefacción = heating
- la cama = bed
- la cocina = kitchen
- el colchón = mattress
- el comedor = dining room
- la cortina = curtain
- la cómoda = chest of drawers
- la estantería = shelf / bookcase
- el frigorífico = fridge
- la habitación = room / bedroom
- el jardín = garden
- la lámpara = lamp
- la lavadora = washing machine
- la pared = wall
- el restaurante = restaurant
- la ropa = clothes
- la silla = chair
- el sofá = sofa
- la ventana = window

Places

- el acuario = aquarium
- las afueras = outskirts
- el ayuntamiento = town hall
- el bar = bar / pub
- la biblioteca = library
- el bosque = forest
- el café = café
- la calle = street
- el carnaval = carnival
- el castillo = castle
- el cine = cinema
- la ciudad = city
- la comedia = comedy
- el concierto = concert
- la costumbre = custom
- el deporte = sport
- la discoteca = nightclub
- el espectáculo = show
- el estadio = stadium
- la estación = station
- a fábrica = factory
- la farmacia = pharmacy
- el festival = festival
- la fiesta = party / celebration
- el gimnasio = gym
- el monumento = monument
- la montaña rusa = roller coaster
- el museo = museum
- la parada de autobús = bus stop
- el parque de atracciones = amusement park
- el parque zoológico = zoo
- la piscina = pool
- el pueblo = village / town
- el restaurante = restaurant
- la taquilla = box office
- el teatro = theater
- el torneo = tournament
- el viaje = trip / journey
- la visita guiada = guided tour

Transport and tourism

- aeropuerto = airport
- albergue juvenil = youth hostel
- alojamiento = accommodation
- andén = platform (railway)
- autobús = bus
- autocar = coach
- avión = plane
- billete (de ida y vuelta) = (single / return) ticket
- calle = street
- coche = car
- crucero = cruise
- destino = destination
- documento de identidad (DNI) = identity card
- embajada = embassy
- equipaje = luggage
- estación de autobuses = bus station
- estación de tren = train station
- extranjero = abroad / foreign country
- guía turístico/guía = tour guidebook
- hacer la maleta = to pack (a suitcase)
- información turística = tourist information
- llegada = arrival
- maleta = suitcase
- mapa = map
- mostrador = check-in desk
- pasaporte = passport
- pasajero = passenger
- permiso de conducir = driving licence
- plataforma = platform
- puerto = port / harbour
- quedarse = to stay
- recoger el equipaje = to collect luggage
- reservar = to book / to reserve
- salida = departure
- seguro de viaje = travel insurance
- taquilla = ticket office
- tarjeta de embarque = boarding pass
- tráfico = traffic
- tren = train
- viaje = trip / journey
- viajar = to travel
- visado = visa
- vuelo = flight

Shopping, clothes, and home goods

- abrigo = coat
- ahorrar = to save
- armario = wardrobe
- bolso = handbag
- bufanda = scarf
- la caja = till / cash register
- el cambio = change / exchange
- camiseta = T-shirt
- carnicería = butcher's
- el centro comercial = shopping centre
- cortina = curtain
- descuento = discount
- devolver = to return
- falda = skirt
- frutería = greengrocer's
- gastar / gasto = to spend / spending
- joyería = jeweller's
- lámpara = lamp
- mercado = market
- mueble = piece of furniture
- pagar = to pay
- panadería = bakery
- pantalón corto = shorts
- paraguas = umbrella
- pastelería = pastry shop
- pescadería = fishmonger's
- probarse = to try on
- rebaja = sale (price reduction)
- regalar = to give a present
- ropa = clothes
- ropa interior = underwear
- ropa deportiva = sportswear
- ropa de cama = bed linen
- sábana = sheet
- tienda = shop
- vestido = dress
- vaqueros = jeans
- zapato = shoe
- zapatillas = trainers

Health and lifestyle

- activo = active
- acostarse = to go to bed
- el ánimo = mood, spirit
- el cuerpo = body
- cansado / cansarse = tired / to get tired
- cuidarse = to take care of oneself
- doler = to hurt
- el dolor = pain / ache
- dormir(se) = to sleep / to fall asleep
- equilibrado = balanced
- la alimentación = diet, nutrition
- comer sano = to eat healthily
- el ejercicio (físico) = (physical) exercise
- la enfermedad = illness
- estar bien/mal = to be well / ill
- estar en forma = to be fit
- estresante = stressing / stressful
- la meditación = meditation
- relajarse = to relax
- la salud = health
- saludable = healthy
- la vida = life

Dialogue examples: daily life and travel

Home

A: Vi un anuncio de un piso en alquiler en las afueras.
(I saw an advert for a flat to rent on the outskirts.)
B: Sí, es una casa adosada; el alquiler es de 500 euros al mes.
(Yes, it's a semi-detached house; the rent is €500 per month.)

A: ¿Dónde puedo aparcar cerca del ayuntamiento?
(Where can I park near the town hall?)
B: Hay un aparcamiento en la calle Mayor, al lado de la biblioteca.
(There's a parking area on Main Street, next to the library.)

A: Estoy ahorrando para comprar una alfombra nueva.
(I'm saving up to buy a new carpet.)
B: Yo también. Mi abrigo estaba a mitad de precio en el centro comercial.
(Me too. My coat was half price at the shopping centre.)

A: En mi piso hay un ascensor, pero no hay armario en el baño.
(My flat has a lift but no wardrobe in the bathroom.)
B: Puedes arreglarlo y poner un armario junto a la cama.
(You can fix that and put a wardrobe next to the bed.)

A: Compré un café con un billete y me dieron dos céntimos de cambio en la caja.
(I bought a coffee with a banknote and they gave me two cents in change at the till.)
B: ¡Genial! Siempre reviso el cambio cuando pago.
(Great! I always check the change when I pay.)

Transport and tourism

A: Quiero un billete de ida y vuelta a Madrid.
(I want a return ticket to Madrid.)
B: Lo puedes comprar en la taquilla o con la agencia de viajes.
(You can buy it at the ticket office or at the travel agent's.)

A: Disculpe, ¿es este el asiento del pasajero con pasaporte 12345?
(Excuse me, is this the seat of the passenger with passport 12345?)
B: Sí, soy yo. Gracias por comprobarlo. *(Yes, it is. Thanks for checking.)*

A: ¿Podemos reservar una habitación doble con media pensión?
(Can we book a double room with half board?)
B: Sí – tenemos pensión completa o media pensión disponibles.
(Yes – we have full board or half board available.)

A: ¿Tienes tu permiso de conducir? *(Do you have your driving licence?)*
B: Sí, está en mi maleta. ¿Quién va a conducir?
(Yes, it's in my suitcase. Who will drive?)
A: Yo, soy el conductor oficial del viaje. *(I will – I'm the official driver of the trip.)*

A: ¿Reservaste los billetes de avión para tu jefa?
(Did you book the airline tickets for your boss)
B: ¡Ah, no, lo olvidé! ¡Ojalá pueda reservar un billete!
(Oh no, I forgot! Hopefully I can still book a ticket now!)

Places

A: Disculpe, ¿cómo llego a la estación de tren desde aquí?
(Excuse me, how do I get to the train station from here?.)
B: Baja por esta calle y gira a la izquierda.
(Go down this street and turn left.)

A: ¿Cuál es tu parte favorita de vivir en tu pueblo?
(What's your favourite part of living in your village?.)
B: Mi pueblo es muy pintoresco y me encantan las pequeñas tiendas de artesanías.
(My village is very quaint and I love the little craft stores.)

Shopping, clothes, and home goods

A: ¿Has visto el descuento del 50 % en esta tienda?
(Have you seen the 50 % discount in this shop?)
B: Sí, voy a comprar ese abrigo y una bufanda.
(Yes, I'm going to buy that coat and a scarf.)

A: Este vestido no me gusta. ¿Puedo devolverlo?
(I don't like this dress. Can I return it?)
B: Claro, con el recibo y la tarjeta de crédito.
(Of course, with the receipt and your credit card.)

A: Voy a la carnicería, la frutería y la panadería.
(I'm going to the butcher's, the greengrocer's, and the bakery.)
B: Entonces pasaré por la pescadería y la pastelería.
(Then I'll drop by the fishmonger's and the pastry shop.)

A: Necesitamos un nuevo mueble para el salón.
(We need a new piece of furniture for the living room.)
B: Hay una rebaja en la tienda de muebles este fin de semana.
(There's a sale at the furniture shop this weekend.)

Health and lifestyle

A: Para estar en forma, debes hacer ejercicio y entrenar.
(To be fit, you must do exercise and train.)
B: Sí, me levanto, me entreno y luego desayuno saludablemente.
(Yes, I get up, train, and then have a healthy breakfast.)

A: Mi trabajo es muy estresante y me canso pronto.
(My job is very stressful and I get tired quickly.)
B: Tómate tiempo para descansar y dormir ocho horas.
(Take time to rest and sleep eight hours.)

A: Me duele el cuerpo después del entrenamiento.
(My body hurts after the training.)
B: Descansa y, si persiste el dolor, consulta al médico.
(Rest, and if the pain persists, see a doctor.)

A: Es tarde; voy a acostarme ya.
(It's late; I'm going to bed now.)
B: Buenas noches. Que te despiertes descansado.
(Good night. Hope you wake up refreshed.)

Theme vocabulary: education and work

School/college life

la academia = academy; post 16 specialist school
académico/a = attentive; scholarly
el acoso = bullying
la agenda = diary
el alumno = pupil; student
aprender = to learn
los apuntes = notes
atento = attentive
el aula = classroom
ausente = absent
ayudar = to help
el bachillerato = baccalaureate
la biblioteca = library
la biología = biology
el bolígrafo = pen
el campo de deportes = sports field
el colegio / la escuela = school
el comportamiento = behaviour
contestar = to answer
charlar = to chat
el chicle = chewing gum
los deberes = homework
desobediente = disobedient
dibujar = to draw
diseñar = to design
educativo = educational
entender = to understand
escribir = to write
el estuche = pencil case
la explicación = explanation
explicar = to explain
faltar = to be absent
el gimnasio = gymnasium
el instituto = secondary school; institute
el intercambio = exchange (pupil)
los lápices de colores = colour pencils
la lección = lesson
leer = to read
la letra = letter (of the alphabet)
levantar la mano = to put your hand up
el libro = book
mirar = to look
la mochila = rucksack; school bag
olestar = to annoy; to bother
el nivel = level
obligatorio = compulsory
oír = to listen; to hear
olvidar = to forget
la página = page
la palabra = word
pasar (la lista) = to call the register
el permiso = permission
la pizarra interactiva = smart board
la pregunta = question
preguntar = to ask a question
privado = private
prometer = to promise; to show promise
la prueba = test; proof
el recreo = break; recess; playtime; recreation
la regla = rule; ruler
repartir = to hand out
repasar = to revise
la respuesta = answer
el resumen = summary
la reunión = meeting
la rutina = routine
la sala de profesores = staffroom
el salón de actos = hall; assembly room
sobresaliente = outstanding
el tema = topic; theme
a tiempo completo = full-time
a tiempo parcial = part-time
tener miedo = to be afraid
terminar = to finish
el trabajo = work; assignment
el trimestre = term / trimester

Subjects and assessment

el alemán = German
aprobar = to pass an exam
el arte dramático = drama
la asignatura = subject
la biología = biology
las ciencias = science
las ciencias económicas = economics
la cocina = food tech
el comercio = business studies
el derecho = law studies
el dibujo = drawing/art
el director = head teacher; principal
enseñar = to teach
el español = Spanish
la evaluación = assessment
el examen = examination
el éxito = success
la expectativa = hope, prospect
la falta = mistake; absence
fracasar = to fail
la filosofía = philosophy
la física = physics
el francés = French
la geografía = geography
la gimnasia = gymnastics
la historia = history
el idioma = language
la informática = IT
el inglés = English
el laboratorio = laboratory
la lengua = language; tongue
la literatura = literature
lograr = to achieve
la música = music
la nota = mark
la optativa = optional
optar = to choose / opt for
probar = to have a go; to try
el proyecto = project
la química = chemistry
la religión = religion
riguroso = severe; harsh
sacar buenas/malas notas = to get good/bad marks
sencillo = simple; easy
suspender = to fail
el taller = workshop
la tarea = task; homework
la tecnología = technology
triunfar = to succeed

Careers and ambitions

el abogado = lawyer, solicitor
el albañil = bricklayer, building worker
el/la ama de casa = housewife
el aprendizaje = apprenticeship, training
el/ella aspirante = applicant, candidate
a azafata = flight attendant
el becario = trainee, intern
el bombero = firefighter
el cajero = bankteller, cashier
el camarero = waiter
el camionero = lorry driver
el carpintero = joiner, carpenter
la carrera = career; profession
el cartero = postman
el contable = accountant
el dependiente = shop assistant
el electricista = electrician
el/la empleado/a = employee, worker
la empresa = company
el enfermero = nurse
el ejecutivo = executive, officer
el escritor = writer
estar en huelga = to be on strike
estar en paro = to be unemployed
la experiencia laboral = work experience
el gerente = manager
el granjero = farmer
el hombre de negocios = businessman
el ingeniero = engineer (civil/mechanical)
el jefe = boss
llegar a ser = to become
l peluquero = hairdresser
el periodismo = journalism
el pintor = painter, artist
el policía = police officer
el psicólogo / la psicóloga = psychologist
solicitar = to apply for
la solicitud = (job) application
soldado = soldier
el sueldo / salario = wages, salary
el teletrabajo = work from home
el título = university degree
tomar un año libre/sabático = to take a gap year
trabajar = to work
el traductor = translator
la vacante = vacancy, open position
el veterinario = veterinary surgeon

Dialogue examples: education and work

School/college life

A: ¿Puedes pasar la lista, por favor? *(Can you call the register, please?)*
B: Claro, voy a repartir las páginas y luego leer los nombres.
(Sure, I'll hand out the pages and then read the names.)

A: Juan está muy desobediente y molesta a sus compañeros.
(Juan is very disobedient and bothers his classmates.)
B: Tenemos que hablar con él sobre su comportamiento.
(We need to speak to him about his behaviour.)

A: ¿Has repasado los apuntes y la explicación del profesor?
(Have you revised the notes and the teacher's explanation?)
B: Sí, pero tengo miedo de suspender el examen.
(Yes, but I'm afraid I'll fail the exam.)

A: En el proyecto, me ocupo de dibujar y de la explicación final.
(For the project, I'm responsible for drawing and the final explanation.)
B: Yo me encargo de escribir la introducción y de contestar las preguntas.
(I'll take care of writing the introduction and answering the questions.)

A: ¿Qué haces en el recreo? *(What do you do at break?)*
B: Juego al fútbol en el campo de deportes o me voy a la sala de profesores a charlar.
(I play football on the sports field or go to the staffroom to chat.)

A: ¿Vas a la academia de derecho? *(Are you going to the law academy?)*
B: Sí, quiero lograr los conocimientos necesarios para ser calificado.
(Yes, I want to acquire the knowledge necessary to be qualified.)

A: Quiero experiencia laboral en una empresa, pero sin abandonar mis estudios.
(I want work experience at a company, but without leaving my studies.)
B: Podrías trabajar a tiempo parcial y entrenar en formación profesional.
(You could work part-time and do vocational training.)

A: ¿Por qué te vas a tomar un año sabático?
(Why are you going to take a gap year?)
B: Para esperar mejores perspectivas y aprender otro idioma.
(To gain better prospects and learn another language.)

A: Mi objetivo es lograr un puesto estable y una buena carrera.
(My aim is to achieve a stable position and a good career.)
B: Para eso necesitas conocimientos y experiencia laboral.
(For that you need knowledge and work experience.)

Subjects and assessments

A: Este año voy a optar por informática y arte dramático.
(This year I'm going to opt for IT and drama.)
B: ¡Qué interesante! Los talleres son optativos y muy útiles.
(How interesting! The workshops are optional and very useful.)

A: El taller de dibujo es muy estricto y riguroso.
(The drawing workshop is very strict and rigorous.)
B: A mí me gusta que sea riguroso – así aprendo más.
(I like it's rigorous – that way I learn more.)

A: Miré la nota del examen de química. *(I looked at my mark for the chemistry exam.)*
B: ¡Enhorabuena! Has sacado muy buenas notas.
(Congratulations! You got very good marks.)

A: Prefiero las ciencias a las ciencias económicas. *(I prefer science over economics.)*
B: La lengua y la química son mis favoritas. *(Language and chemistry are my favourites.)*

A: Entré en el despacho del director para pedir ayuda con la tarea.
(I went into the head teacher's office to ask for help with the task.)
B: Él me explicó la lección de forma muy sencilla y clara.
(He explained the lesson to me in a very simple and clear way.)

Careers and ambitions

A: Quiero ser veterinario porque me encantan los animales.
(I want to be a vet because I love animals.)
B: ¡Genial! ¿Vas a estudiar mucho para tu título?
(Great! Are you going to study hard for your degree?)

A: Hola, soy Juan, solicito información para un aprendiz de electricista.
(Hi, I'm Juan; I'm applying for an electrician apprenticeship.)
B: Encantada. Rellena esta solicitud y hablaremos de horas de trabajo flexibles.
(Nice to meet you. Fill in this application and we'll discuss flexi-time.)

A: ¿Cuál es el sueldo para un periodista recién graduado?
(What's the salary for a newly graduated journalist?)
B: Sobre 1 800 € al mes, pero puedes triunfar y "subir de nivel."
(About €1,800 monthly, but you can succeed and "move up the ranks.")

A: ¿Por qué debería contratarle como cartero? *(Why should we hire you as a postman?)*
B: Soy muy responsable, me encargo de mi ruta con objetivo de entrega al cien por cien.
(I'm very reliable, I take charge of my route with the aim of 100 % delivery.)

A: Hoy los obreros están en huelga. *(Today the workmen are on strike.)*
B: Sí – protestan por mejores horas de trabajo y un mayor beneficio salarial.
(Yes – they're protesting for better working hours and higher wages.)

Theme vocabulary: the wider world

Celebrations, festivals, and customs

Año Nuevo = New Year
aniversario = anniversary
bandera = flag
boda = wedding
carnaval = carnival
Día de los Inocentes = 28 December (similar to April Fools' Day)
Día de los Muertos = All Souls' Day / Day of the Dead
Día de Reyes = Epiphany (6 January)
día festivo = public holiday
disfraz / disfrazarse de = costume / to dress up as
feria = fair
fiesta = festival / party
fuegos artificiales = fireworks
fecha patria = national day
nacimiento = nativity scene
Navidad = Christmas
Nochebuena = Christmas Eve
Nochevieja = New Year's Eve (31 December)
Papá Noel = Father Christmas / Santa Claus
Pascua = Easter
paso = statue carried in an Easter procession
procesión = procession
quinceañera = fifteenth-birthday celebration (Latin American tradition)
Reyes Magos = the Three Kings / Wise Men
Semana Santa = Holy Week (Easter week)
Tomatina = tomato-throwing festival (Buñol, Spain)
traje típico = traditional costume
villancico = Christmas carol

Technology and the internet

adjuntar = to attach
actualizar = to update
aplicación (app) = application / app
archivo = file
buscador = search engine
clave = key / code (often used for password)
contraseña = password
correo electrónico = email
cortar y pegar = cut and paste
descargar = to download
desactivar = to disable / to block (screen)
enlace = link
herramienta = tool
impresora = printer
inalámbrico = wireless
internauta = Internet user
marcar / marcador = to bookmark
memoria USB = USB stick
mensaje = message
navegador = browser
nube = cloud (computing)
ordenador = computer
página web = webpage
portátil = laptop
portada = homepage
ratón = mouse
red social = social network
reproductor = player / widget
servidor = server
servidor de seguridad = firewall
sitio web = website
subir = to upload
tableta = tablet
teclado = keyboard
usuario = user
wifi = Wi-Fi

Environment and social issues

agotar = to exhaust / to use up
el agujero = hole
amenazar = to threaten
apagar = to turn off
el asilo = asylum / care home
el atasco = traffic jam
el aumento = increase
el beneficio = benefit
la capa de ozono = ozone layer
el calentamiento global = global warming
el cambio climático = climate change
combatir = to fight / to combat
el consumo = consumption
la contaminación = pollution
el contaminante = pollutant
los desechos = waste / rubbish
el desperdicio = waste / squandering
la desigualdad = inequality
el derecho = right (human right)
el desempleo = unemployment
el desarrollo sostenible = sustainable development
el efecto invernadero = greenhouse effect
la energía renovable = renewable energy
ensuciar = to make dirty
el envase = packaging / container
la escasez = shortage / lack
estropear = to ruin / to spoil
los gases de escape = exhaust fumes
la huelga = strike
el huracán = hurricane
la igualdad = equality
la inmigración = immigration
la inundación = flood
la justicia = justice
la lluvia ácida = acid rain
la marea negra (vertido de petróleo) = oil spill
la multa = fine / penalty
nocivo = harmful
la obra benéfica = charity (project)
la ONG = NGO (non-governmental organisation)
el petróleo = oil
el prejuicio = prejudice
recaudar fondos = to raise funds
el reciclaje = recycling
los recursos naturales = natural resources
los residuos = refuse / waste
el río = river
la selva = jungle / tropical forest
la sequía = drought
personas sin hogar = homeless people
el testigo = witness
el vertedero = rubbish dump
voluntario / voluntaria = volunteer